Insects of Eastern...

D. H. Walker and A. R. Pittaway

Illustrated by A. J. Walker

MACMILLAN PUBLISHERS

© Text D. H. Walker and A. R. Pittaway 1987
© Illustrations A. J. Walker 1987

First published 1987

All rights reserved. No reproduction, copy or transmission of this publication may be made without written permission. No paragraph of this publication may be reproduced, copied or transmitted save with written permission or in accordance with the provisions of the Copyright Act 1956 (as amended). Any person who does any unauthorised act in relation to this publication may be liable to criminal prosecution and civil claims for damages.

Published by Macmillan Publishers Ltd
London and Basingstoke
Associated companies and representatives in Accra, Auckland, Delhi, Dublin, Gaborone, Hamburg, Harare, Hong Kong, Kuala Lumpur, Lagos, Manzini, Melbourne, Mexico City, Nairobi, New York, Singapore, Tokyo

ISBN 0-333-43214-2

Design by Milford Hurley Graphic Design

Printed Hong Kong

Contents

Foreword	iv
Preface	v
Acknowledgements	vi
Scope	vii
Introduction	viii
Classification	ix
The anatomy of insects	xv
Insect orders:	
Thysanura (Bristletails)	2
Odonata (Dragonflies & Damselflies)	3
Orthoptera (Crickets & Grasshoppers)	12
Dermaptera (Earwigs)	23
Dictyoptera (Cockroaches & Mantises)	24
Isoptera (Termites)	28
Psocoptera (Booklice)	30
Mallophaga (Biting Lice)	30
Anoplura (Sucking Lice)	31
Hemiptera (True Bugs, Cicadas, Plant Hoppers & Aphids)	32
Thysanoptera (Thrips)	42
Neuroptera (Lacewings & Antlions)	43
Lepidoptera (Moths & Butterflies)	48
Diptera (True Flies)	101
Siphonaptera (Fleas)	111
Hymenoptera (Bees, Wasps, Ants & Ichneumon Wasps)	112
Coleoptera (Beetles)	129
Appendix: A new species of Mydaidae (Midas Flies)	153
Reflections on Arabia	155
Bibliography	162
Index of scientific names	165
Index of common names	171

Foreword

by Prince Abdullah Bin Faisal Bin Turki

In the summer of 1980 I attended a dinner party in Riyadh and during the course of the evening I had the opportunity to view a small collection of insects from Saudi Arabia that was on display. The exhibition demonstrated the diversity and beauty of the insect life found in the Kingdom. Don Walker, the organiser of the exhibition and a keen entomologist, had spent much time visiting localities in central and eastern Saudi Arabia collecting insects. He was of the opinion that the country contained a great number of species that had not yet been recorded and that it would make a very interesting study for anyone who wanted an activity to occupy their spare time. However, the number of publications available to assist the amateur enthusiast was limited and so it was Don's intention to publish a book on the subject.

The scope of such a book was extensive and the many new records required correct identification. Don formed a liaison with a young entomologist, Tony Pittaway, who was also working in the Kingdom. Tony contributed his records to the total available and then carried out extensive research at the British Museum in London to identify and classify specimens. Both authors thought that the book should have a universal appeal, especially to families, so that it could be used by both parents and children. They were anxious that the book should capture the beauty of the insects and the magic of the country where the insects lived. With this in mind the text includes scenes and situations within the habitat of the insects. Furthermore, it was decided not to use photographs but to enlist the help of an artist, Allan Walker, who could impart these impressions into the book. He visited Saudi Arabia in 1981, when a number of his superb illustrations were drawn on location.

I am happy to have had an association with this publication and I think it will have a general appeal both to Saudi nationals and to visiting expatriates.

عبدالله بن فيصل بن تركي العبدالله السعود

ABDULLAH BIN FAISAL BIN TURKI AL-ABDULLAH AL-SAUD
Riyadh

Preface

No nightingale did ever chaunt
  More welcome notes to weary bands
Of travellers in some shady haunt,
  Among Arabian sands.

> WILLIAM WORDSWORTH, 1770–1850
> *The Solitary Reaper*

For centuries mankind has viewed Arabia through romantic eyes, as a land of deep contrasts, where a hostile environment challenged the survival of those seeking the beauty and riches that lay hidden. It was known that in the depths of the vast deserts were places of great beauty and tranquillity.

The key to the location of shady haunts was water; where water was, life flourished. Here were to be found beautiful groves of trees bearing many different types of fruit, lush green vegetation, unique animals, colourful birds and countless insects, each with its duty to perform in the ecological web of life.

Today this is still true and, with the rich discovery of oil, man can now afford to extend his use of water. Many insects have benefited from the increase in the number of localities available to them. However, most are adapted in their shapes and habits for survival in the original desert environment. This book is a guide to the unusual and often beautiful insect life of Arabia.

> D. H. WALKER
> A. R. PITTAWAY

Acknowledgements

This book was prompted by a love for the beauty and freedom of the desert. The majority of the contents of the book are records from a happy association with this environment. Consequently, our first thoughts go to the people of Arabia whom we met while collecting this information. We wish to thank them for their help and unfailing hospitality. We are also very grateful for the assistance given by Prince Abdullah Bin Faisal Bin Turki without whose encouragement this book would never have been written.

To obtain information and to identify species it was often necessary to consult specialists. We wish to thank the following for their help: R. Arora, P. Barnhard, J. Bowden, M. Brendell, S. Brooks, B. Cogan, R. Daly, M. Day, W. Dolling, G. Else, P. Freeman (Keeper BMNH), P. Gilbert, K. Guichard, A. Hayes, W. Al-Houty, T. Huddleston, L. Jessop, T. B. Larsen, J. Marshall, G. Popov, C. Vardy, E. Wiltshire.

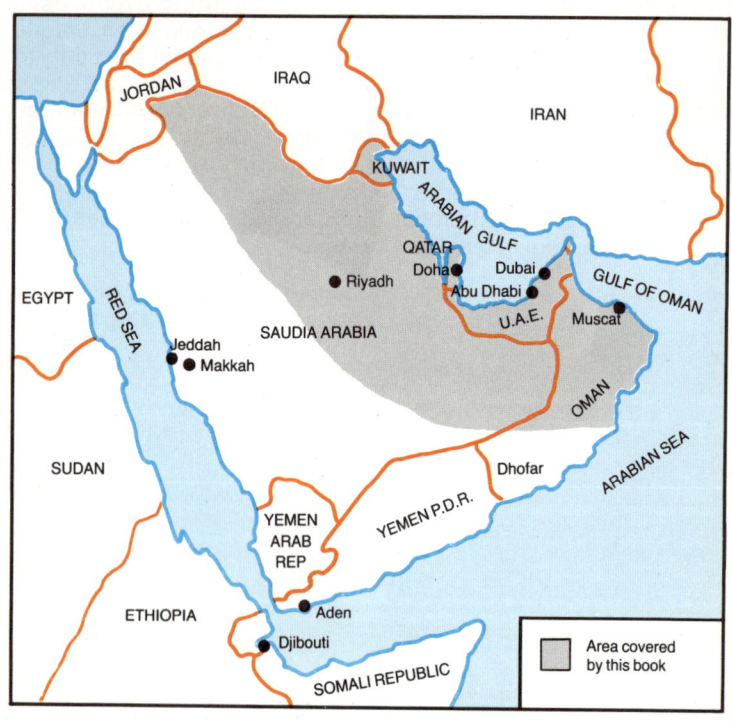

Scope

The region of Arabia covered by this book is shown shaded on the map on p. vi. This area is bounded in the north by Iraq, the Najd Plateau to the west, the Ar Rub Al Khali (Empty Quarter) to the south and the Arabian Gulf (as far as the Arabian Sea) to the east. The exact number of insect species that live in the region is not known, as large areas remain unexplored entomologically and new discoveries continue to occur. The insects covered by this book are given in the Index of Scientific Names (pp. 165 – 170). The scientific names are used because the common names (pp. 171 – 175) are arbitrary, the result of personal choice and often very ambiguous. However, the book does not include those insects that are so minute that they are barely visible to the human eye. The illustrations include a representative species from most of the major families that occur within the region and these species were generally chosen as those most likely to be encountered. The months of the year when the insect is generally in its adult stage are given below the small-scale map depicting the known range of the species. The illustrations include some of the foodplants and habitats in which the insects are found.

An important feature of this book is that most of the insects appear life size. Where this is not the case magnifications are given as, for example, × 1.5, indicating the illustration is one and a half times life size. Many of the sexes are indistinguishable but where there are important differences the sexes are distinguished as male (♂) or female (♀).

Introduction

Shimmering in the heat, the view from the top of the sand dune was extensive. Across the summit a warm wind blew the fine particles into ridges like waves on a beach. One's eyes relaxed as they explored the horizon; extending in all directions, the Al Dahna was a delight of rolling sand and stone hillocks, a patchwork of moving shadows created by fleeting clouds. Below, an island of barely green steppe, some five kilometres long and one kilometre wide, struggled for survival awaiting the rain to bring life again to the gaunt and bare Mimosa (*Acacia*). Half a dozen black bedouin tents stood a quarter of a kilometre apart and their attendant sheep savoured the last vestige of vegetation left by a merciless sun. In the cool dark recesses beneath the rocks other life existed; the insects. These animals had also discovered how to survive and to contribute to the evolution of life in this challenging land.

Insects belong to a large phylum or division of the animal kingdom called the Arthropoda. These have common characteristics, which include jointed legs, an external skeleton, 'cold blood' and a specialised excretory system. Their structure encourages the conservation of water in the body which helps them to survive in severe climatic conditions. The Arthropoda contain the following classes:

1. Insecta (Insects).
2. Arachnida (Spiders, Scorpions and Mites).
3. Crustacea (Crabs, Lobsters and Woodlice).
4. Myriapoda (Centipedes and Millipedes).

Insects are the only class of Arthropoda to have wings, although not all insects have wings. However, all insects have 3 body divisions and never have more than 3 pairs of true legs. Insects are a highly successful form of life. They are the largest class of multicellular animals in the world and account for over three-quarters of the known species. Throughout most of the world, they have adapted their habits to survive on land, where they utilise a vast variety of food sources. Most insects are small in size. This is due to limitations dictated by the respiratory system. (Oxygen is obtained direct from the air through passages leading to the tissues.) They carry out countless necessary functions and life as we know it today would not exist without their contribution.

Classification

One of the major problems when studying insects is communication, that is, being quite certain that everyone is referring to the same thing, regardless of language barriers. During the eighteenth century an attempt was made to achieve this for biology by the Swedish naturalist Linnaeus. He introduced a classification scheme upon which the present-day system is based. This system groups under separate headings all living matter. The full name given to an individual species relates it to other individual species which have similar characteristics. The names generally originate from Latin, a dead language which is less prone to misinterpretation and is acceptable throughout the world. In this book the universal system has been adopted, but at the same time reference has been made to some English names, since they are in common usage. These are shown in parentheses, for example *Papilio demoleus* L. (Citrus Swallowtail).

The schematic diagram shows how the system operates in classifying the insects found in this book. Definitions of the terms used in this system are given below:

ANIMAL	A living creature which has the faculty of perception or feeling and the ability to make voluntary motion. Not a plant.
ARTHROPODA	A phylum of animals with jointed limbs and an external skeleton.
INSECTA	A class of Arthropoda embracing animals that have 3 body divisions and 3 pairs of legs. Insecta also includes all of the Arthropoda species that have developed wings.
APTERYGOTA	A subclass of primitive insects that have never developed wings. The young insects resemble a modified adult insect.
PTERYGOTA	A subclass of more advanced insects which in the majority of cases have developed wings.
EXOPTERYGOTA	A division of pterygote insects containing insects whose life-cycle does not include a complete metamorphosis, i.e. pupal stage of development. The young insects resemble the adult. The wings, when present, develop externally.

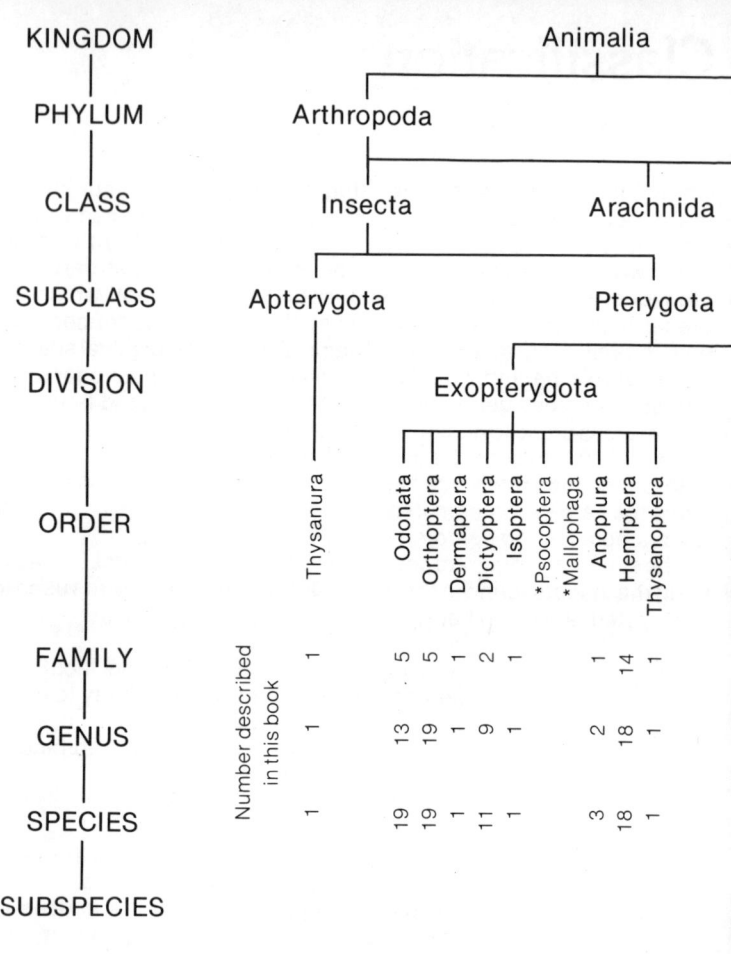

	ENDOPTERYGOTA	A division of pterygote insects which have a complete metamorphosis, and the wings, when present, develop inside the body.
	THYSANURA	An order of apterygote insects which includes Silverfish.
	ODONATA	An order of exopterygote insects which includes Dragonflies.
	ORTHOPTERA	An order of exopterygote insects which includes Crickets and Grasshoppers.
	DERMAPTERA	An order of exopterygote insects which includes Earwigs.

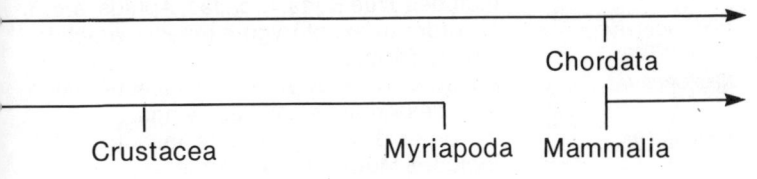

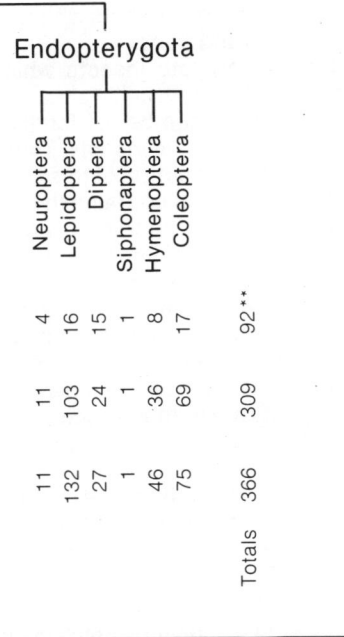

Neuroptera	Lepidoptera	Diptera	Siphonaptera	Hymenoptera	Coleoptera	
4	16	15	1	8	17	92**
11	103	24	1	36	69	309
11	132	27	1	46	75	366
						Totals

*These orders are not represented in this book.
**Includes superfamilies

DICTYOPTERA	An order of exopterygote insects which includes Cockroaches and Mantises.
ISOPTERA	An order of exopterygote insects which includes Termites.
PSOCOPTERA	An order of exopterygote insects which includes Booklice.
MALLOPHAGA	An order of exopterygote insects which includes Biting Lice.
ANOPLURA	An order of exopterygote insects which includes Sucking Lice.

HEMIPTERA	An order of exopterygote insects which includes True Bugs, Cicadas, Aphids, etc.
THYSANOPTERA	An order of exopterygote insects which includes Thrips.
NEUROPTERA	An order of endopterygote insects which includes Antlions and Lacewings.
LEPIDOPTERA	An order of endopterygote insects which includes Moths and Butterflies.
DIPTERA	An order of endopterygote insects which includes True Flies.
SIPHONAPTERA	An order of endopterygote insects which includes Fleas.
HYMENOPTERA	An order of endopterygote insects which includes Wasps, Ants and Bees.
COLEOPTERA	An order of endopterygote insects which includes Beetles.
FAMILIES	Each order contains a number of families which group together similar insects. These families are listed in the section of this book devoted to the order which contains them.
GENUS	Further classification within the individual families is achieved by grouping together insects that have very similar characteristics and assigning them to the same genus (plural 'genera'). The genera are shown with the specific names under the appropriate family.
SPECIES	Collections of animals which are capable of interbreeding freely are termed species. For identification, an insect should always be referred to by both the name of its genus and its specific name. A checklist of the species of insects included in this book is given on pp. 165 – 170. Reference is also made to individual species in the section that describes the order to which they belong.
NAME	The name following the specific name is the author of the specific name. This is often abbreviated, e.g. L. means Linnaeus.
SUBSPECIES	In some instances, groups of the same species may be isolated geographically from one another to such an extent that they do not have the opportunity to interbreed. If their environment differs they may develop in a dissimilar manner and acquire distinctive recognisable characteristics. In such cases, it is not unusual to assign a name to the subspecies to denote the insect's origin.

SUPERFAMILIES

It should be noted that it is still possible for members of different subspecies to interbreed.

Where there is a large number of families in an order, the term 'superfamilies' is often used to group together families with similar characteristics. For example, in this book it occurs in the order Hemiptera, which is divided into the following two superfamilies:

Heteroptera containing 11 families.
Homoptera containing 3 families.

Take the following as an example:

High above the escarpment, a lone vulture sailed effortlessly in the clear blue sky, the only sign of life in a land of sunbaked rocks. A dry wadi led into the valley below, where a small farm lay hidden from sight; a green oasis of date palms in the barren desert. Upon entering the trees one could hear the quiet hum of insect life and the rich fluty song of the Bulbul, while the distant thump, thump of a diesel pump soon became apparent. Occasional shafts of sunlight found their way through the thick foliage to provide areas of brightness in the damp shade. The ground was covered with a short, tough grass and littered with overripe dates. A number of small fig trees and a banana plant lined an irrigation watercourse. Several large, yellow and black butterflies flew with powerful flight among the trees. From time to time they settled on the pink flowers of Sweet Basil where their beauty was displayed to advantage. A careful inspection revealed that there were two different types of butterfly, although they looked alike in flight. They were identified as the Citrus Swallowtail and the Common Swallowtail. To describe these species, the established classification system could be used as follows:

Kingdom	Animalia
Phylum	Arthropoda
Class	Insecta
Subclass	Pterygota
Division	Endopterygota
Order	Lepidoptera (Butterflies)
Family	Papilionidae (Swallowtails)
Genus	*Papilio*
Species (I)	*demoleus* L. (Citrus Swallowtail)
Species (II)	*machaon* L. (Common Swallowtail)
Subspecies (II)	*syriacus* Verity

From this system, the relationship of the two butterflies is clear, and their similarity to each other is indicated, since they both belong to the same genus. Both insects have a powerful flight and are capable of travelling long distances. The Citrus Swallowtail has extended its range from India across Iran to Arabia. There are no striking differences between specimens from different localities in the Middle East and the name *Papilio demoleus* is therefore considered adequate to identify this insect. The Common Swallowtail also has a wide range, and occurs throughout Europe, North Africa and Asia to Canada. Under favourable conditions it will extend its range, but normally is confined to favoured areas that contain the foodplant of the larvae. The form of the insect that is found in southern Sweden is considered to be the normal or 'type', and is named *Papilio machaon machaon*. A number of recognisably different forms of the same insect occur; the one found in Saudi Arabia is named *Papilio machaon syriacus*, while the one found in Britain is named *Papilio machaon britannicus* — thus providing an identity to the origin of a particular Common Swallowtail butterfly.

Tarut Island, one of the many cultivated oases in Eastern Saudi Arabia

The Anatomy of Insects

The anatomy of all adult insects conforms to the image of an 'Original Insect' which may have existed during prehistoric times. Most insects have the same number of limbs and organs as this Original Insect, although the shape and function of a particular limb or organ might have changed during evolution to enable the present-day insect to adapt to their environment or food source. In some cases, present-day insects have lost original limbs or organs as these have become either unnecessary or a hindrance to their specific life-styles.

All insects have a tough external skeleton called the cuticle. This contains a nitrogenous polysaccharide, known as chitin, whose hardness and flexibility varies to suit the requirements of the limb or organ of the insect. The external surface is covered with a wax which renders it waterproof and helps the insect to retain moisture. The exoskeleton of the Original Insect was considered to have been roughly cylindrical and made up of 20 segments. This contained internal organs and external appendages required to convert food into energy, to reproduce the species and to control the activities of the insect.

The present-day insect *Blatta orientalis* (Common Cockroach) is generally considered to bear a close resemblance to the Original Insect. The anatomy of this insect comprises 3 main parts: the head, the thorax and the abdomen. The head is made up of 6 segments which are fused together to form a strong skull. Excellent vision is provided by 2 compound eyes and three ocelli, or simple eyes, which are situated on the head. The antennae are attached to the head and are sensitive to vibration and smell. The head also contains the mouth, which is equipped with 2 pairs of external jaws (the mandibles) and maxillae. Food is chewed externally before entering the mouth. Two pairs of small appendages are situated close to the mouth – the maxillary and labial palps. Their function is to provide taste and to ascertain the suitability of the food. Within the mouth a small appendage, the hypopharynx, discharges saliva from the salivary glands to assist digestion.

The thorax is the second main part of the insect and is formed from 3 segments: the prothorax, the mesothorax and the metathorax. Each of these segments is provided with 1 pair of legs. Both the mesothorax and the metathorax may support 1 pair of wings.

The third main part of the insect is the abdomen and this comprises 11 segments which have only a few openings or appendages. One main opening is the anus, which is situated at the rear of the abdomen and is used to dispose of waste products. Above the anus there is a pair of sensory appendages called cerci. A further pair of sexual appendages is situated on the male which are not present on the female.

A detailed description of the internal anatomy of insects is beyond the scope of this book and the following comments are only intended as an introduction. One long blood vessel runs through the centre of the insect and connects each segment. There are no capillary blood vessels, so this central vessel acts as the heart. It is surrounded by tissue bathed in blood. Contraction of the walls creates flow through openings in the vessel. The tissues obtain oxygen by absorption from the air which finds its way from the external surface along minute tubes. A central nervous system exists connecting the organs and extremities to a nerve centre situated along the entire body length as a series of ganglia.

Food, after entering the mouth, passes into the crop where saliva starts the digestive process. From the crop it enters the gizzard, where it is thoroughly chewed by a number of teeth. The finely ground food is then filtered through a sieve of hairs to the gut where the insect extracts its requirements. Unwanted products of digestion travel along the intestine and are excreted through the anus. The reproductive organs are also situated in the abdomen.

A remote part of the Tuwayq Hills in Central Saudi Arabia where the ancient Acacia trees attract large numbers of insects and many species of birds

Insect Orders

Thysanura
(Bristletails)

Bristletails are classified as apterygote (wingless) insects. This subclass is generally considered to be the most primitive order of insects in existence. Fossil remains have been discovered in Scotland of an animal that bears a very close resemblance to these insects, in rocks of the Devonian Period which are over 300 million years old. All other known fossil insects are more advanced and are from more recent rock formations. The Bristletail is a carrot-shaped insect less than 2 cm in length, covered in scales, with 2 long thin antennae and 3 'tails', and no wings or vestige of wings. The life-cycle does not include a pronounced metamorphosis; the young insects resemble the adult except in size, and moulting and growth continues well into maturity. There are a number of species to be found in Arabia some of which live as guests in the nests of *Cataglyphis* ants. Most look similar and identification is a specialist operation beyond the scope of this book.

Lepismatidae (Silverfish)

JANUARY – DECEMBER

***Thermobia domestica* Packard** (Firebrat) The firebrat is nocturnal but the most likely member of this family to be seen. It is normally found under stones and debris, although it often inhabits houses. Truly a species of the area, it enjoys a warm climate, but has also adapted to life in more temperate zones by selected habitation in bakehouses and kitchens. It feeds on vegetable and household debris.

× 1·5

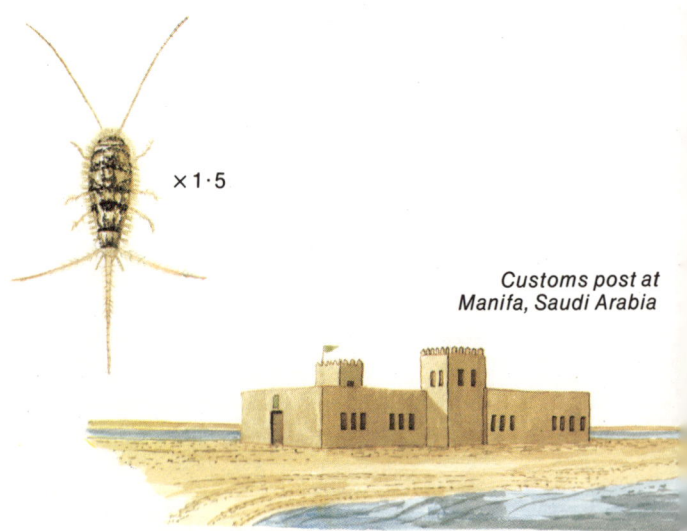

Customs post at Manifa, Saudi Arabia

Odonata
(Dragonflies & Damselflies)

Dragonflies are an order of primitive, usually day-flying insects which have been in existence for approximately 300 million years. The largest known insect is a fossil dragonfly, *Meganeura monyi* Brongniart, from the Upper Carboniferous Period, which had a wingspan of 700 mm (over 2 ft) and was flying in the great swamps long before the arrival of the dinosaurs. Although dragonflies of such giant proportions are not known to exist today, the present insects do not differ appreciably in shape or structure from their ancestors.

Dragonflies are generally found in the vicinity of water and during the larval stage of their development they are aquatic. The adult insect can be a strong migrant, which is the reason why very few stretches of water exist without a dragonfly in attendance. During the day they only fly in sunny weather, when territorial, aerial fights may occur between rivals.

The mating procedure is unusual. The male genitalia are situated in the usual position on the ninth segment, but before mating occurs the male transfers sperm to a special pouch which is situated on the second and third segment. The male then goes in search of a female. (Preliminary courtship occurs among damselflies, but this does not take place with dragonflies.) The male approaches the female who is grasped behind the head by the male claspers. The female's body curves round so that the reproductive organs can collect the sperm from the pouch. The pair then often fly in tandem and certain species remain so even while the female is laying eggs. Some species scatter them on the water, whereas others use their ovipositor to cut a slit in aquatic plants and then insert the egg in the incision. Females have been observed to climb 500 mm (over 1 ½ ft) down a plant below the surface of the water before laying the egg. They have done this with the male still attached and the whole operation has taken over an hour beneath the surface of the water.

The larva that hatches is known as a nymph and is adapted to breathe under water. This period of development can last from 1 to 5 years according to the type of species. During this stage, wing buds form, but there is no pupal stage. When the nymph finally leaves the water the change into an adult includes the completion of the wing formation. This type of life-cycle is termed an 'incomplete metamorphosis'.

Dragonflies are carnivorous both in the immature and adult stages of their lives and their bodies are specially adapted to capture prey. The nymphs eat large quantities of aquatic insects and even small fish. They are also cannibalistic. The nymph can swim; dragonflies use a form of jet propulsion, utilising the water that they suck in and discharge for breathing, while damselflies swim by jerking their bodies. However, their movement is slow and of little use in catching prey, so they rely on a limb called a mask for their hunting. The mask is attached to the lower lip to form a hinged arm, the end of which has claws. The nymph may stalk its prey, then with the use of powerful muscles shoots the mask forward to grasp and withdraw the victim to the mouth, where it is eaten alive.

The adult dragonfly is extremely manoeuvrable in flight and is capable of hovering, hawking and darting. It has large compound eyes that provide excellent vision so it can catch other insects in flight. Its legs face forward to form a basket which grasp and hold the victim while it is being eaten. In the past people have taken care to avoid these formidable yet beautiful creatures, as it was thought that they could sting. However, dragonflies cannot sting and are harmless to human beings.

The order contains two main suborders — Zygoptera (Damselflies) and Anisoptera (Dragonflies). Damselflies are normally more delicate in structure than dragonflies. They have hindwings of a similar shape to the forewings and when not in flight the insect folds these vertically above the body. The eyes of a damselfly are situated on the opposite sides of the head and do not meet. Dragonflies have hindwings which are broad at the base and when not in flight are laid flat at right angles to the body. Also, the 2 huge eyes, one on either side of the head, generally meet at the centre.

The identification of different species of adult dragonflies by coloration may be complicated by several factors. Newly emerged specimens can be of a different colour to more mature specimens. The colour of a male can be different from that of a female of the same species and colours usually fade very rapidly after death.

Zygoptera (Damselflies)
Platycnemididae (Enigmatic Damselflies)

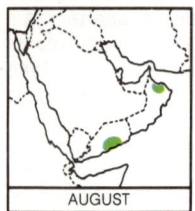
AUGUST

***Arabicnemis caerulea* Waterston** (Powderblue Damselfly) A local species only recently discovered in Northern Oman where it occurs in small numbers in a few limited areas of the Jabal Akhdar and the United Arab Emirates. Frequents rock-face gullies with water and is only found in small groups, which chase each other over the water surface and among the low vegetation.

A stream surrounded by the endemic Muscat Oleander, Jebel Akhdar, Northern Oman

Coenagriidae (Banded Damselflies)

JANUARY – AUGUST

***Ischnura evansi* Morton** (Blue-banded Ishnura) A common species throughout the area. It is found at most shallow pools where the water is shaded, clear and contains emergent vegetation. During March and April large numbers migrate north and are then often found in gardens. These mass movements are generally nocturnal and the insects are often attracted to lighted windows.

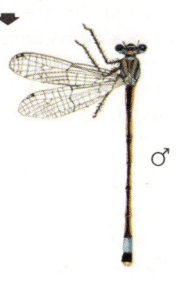
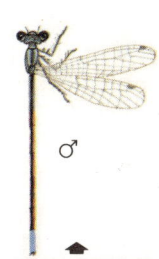

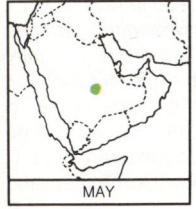

MAY

***Enallagma vansomereni* Pinhey** (Layla Damselfly) An essentially African species, discovered for the first time in the Arabian peninsula at Layla Lakes, Central Saudi Arabia by D. H. Walker. Although little is known of its behaviour, the majority were found amongst new vegetation at the water's edge.

MAY – JULY

***Ceriagrion glabrum* Burmeister** (Olive Eyes) Only found in Northern Oman to date, it frequents small trickles of water situated in large rocky wadis near oases. The dull orange colour acts as an effective camouflage when it flies slowly among the low vegetation.

Anisoptera (Dragonflies)
Gomphidae (Wide-eyed Dragonflies)

APRIL – AUGUST

***Lindenia tetraphylla* van der Linden** (Arabian Lobetail) A strong migrant which is widespread throughout Arabia. Often found by open desert pools, but prefers stretches of water among boulders on the floor of rocky wadis especially those with fringing tamarisk thickets. It will often perch on a favourite stone, suddenly taking off to skim the surface of the water and returning a few minutes later to continue its surveillance. **A**

Aeshnidae (Hawker Dragonflies)

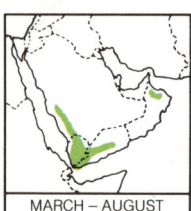

MARCH – AUGUST

***Anax imperator* Leach** (Emperor Dragonfly) Powerful and fast-flying. To date only recorded in eastern Arabia from the mountains of northern Oman. Common in Europe and Britain where it frequents most rivers and streams. Members of the family Aeshnidae generally spend their time hunting for prey, mounting regular patrols along favoured routes. *A. imperator* prefers to patrol rocky rivers, edges of plantations or banks of wild figs which fringe wadis. When at rest, members of the family Aeshnidae suspend themselves among the foliage of a convenient tree or shrub, but never perch. Perching is the rest habit of the family Libellulidae (Darter Dragonflies). **B**

OCTOBER – MAY

***Anax parthenope* Sélys** (Lesser Emperor) Large, powerful and fast-flying. Widespread in Arabia. Flies around open saltmarshes, mangrove swamps, fringes of oases and large desert pools, where it generally hunts flies which it eats while in flight. Migrates in March and April. Occasionally swarms occur in suburbs of towns or on desert farms, when large numbers may be seen hawking around open areas. It is very aggressive and has been known to intercept and chase away large birds. **C**

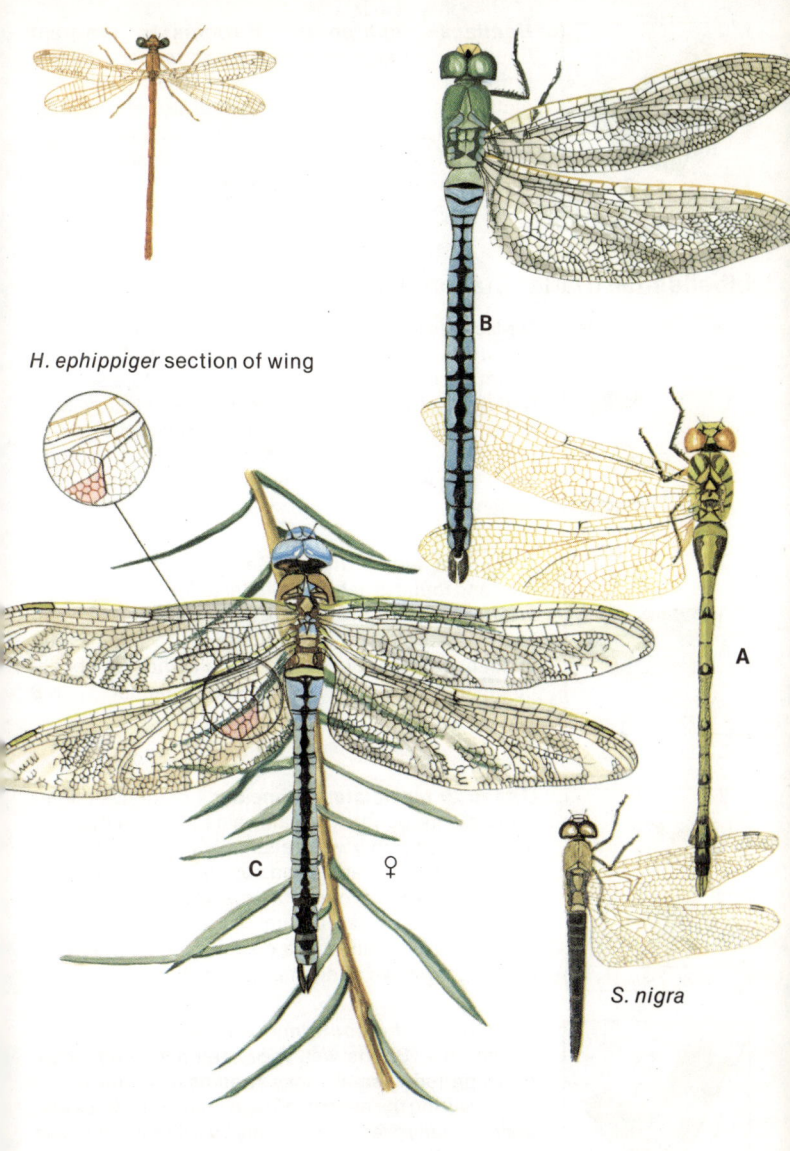

H. ephippiger section of wing

7

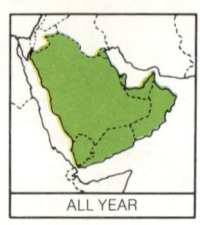

ALL YEAR

***Hemianax ephippiger* Burmeister** (Vagrant Emperor) Very similar to *Anax parthenope* (Lesser Emperor), it requires an expert to identify each correctly. Has 3 'vertical' cells in central area of hindwing, whereas *A. parthenope* has 2 'vertical' cells in this area (see illustration on p. 7). Prefers to inhabit saltmarshes and extensive reed beds near saltflats.

Libellulidae (Darter Dragonflies)

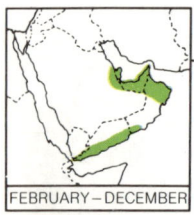

FEBRUARY – DECEMBER

***Diplacodes lefebvrei* Rambur** (Purple Darter) Frequents oases and overgrown riverbanks. Males are a bright purple colour, females and immature adults a buff and dark brown colour, resembling *Selysiothemis nigra* (Desert Darter). All share the normal behaviour of most Libellulidae, which is to perch on top of a prominent twig waiting for likely prey to fly within darting distance. **A**

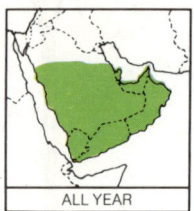

ALL YEAR

***Orthetrum sabina* Drury** (Oasis Skimmer) Common and found in habitats similar to *Diplacodes lefebvrei* (Purple Darter), although its behaviour is very different. Rarely perches, but prefers to hang partly suspended from a bush or grass stalk when not engaged on hunting patrols along a water channel. **B**

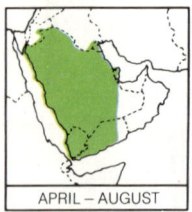

APRIL – AUGUST

***Orthetrum taeniolatum* Schneider** (Azure Skimmer) To date, only found in the Qatif oasis and Kuwait, where it frequents narrow water channels with barren steep banks. Irrigation canals and concrete water tanks on desert farms are favourite haunts, where it patrols the water surface. Female and immature adults are almost identical, but adult males develop a pale grey-blue bloom a few days after emergence. **C**

MARCH – OCTOBER

***Orthetrum chrysostigma* Burmeister** (Girdled Skimmer) Shuns well-vegetated and shady locations, preferring small rocky streams in mountainous areas. During the heat of the day most individuals rest under a shady overhang and only fly if disturbed. Looks similar to *O. taeniolatum* (Azure Skimmer), but ranges rarely overlap. May be distinguished from latter by a restriction which girdles the upper abdomen. **D**

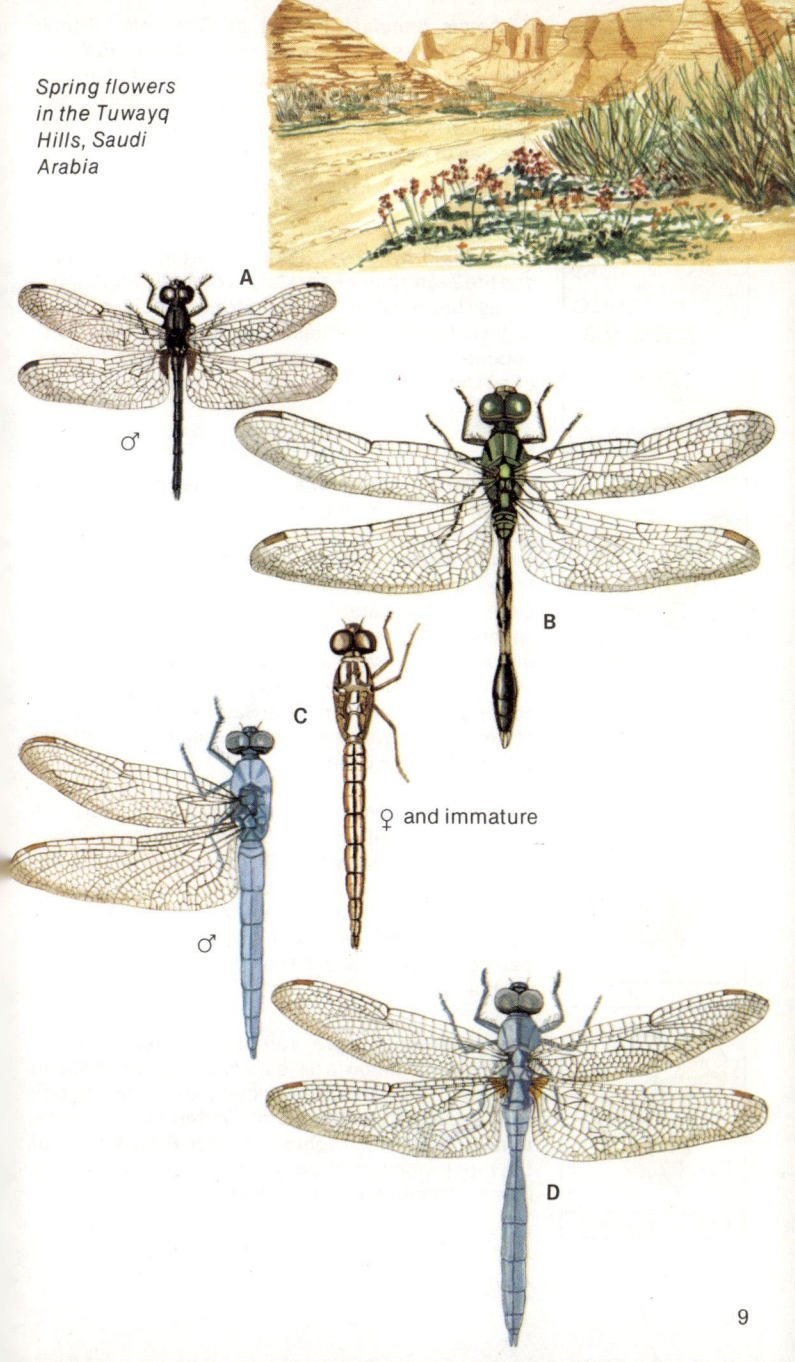

Spring flowers in the Tuwayq Hills, Saudi Arabia

MARCH – DECEMBER

***Trithemis annulata* Palisot de Beauvois** (Purple Blushed Darter)   Very common. Mature male unmistakable with its bright red body. Large numbers may be found around reedbeds and riverbanks. They defend their territory against all-comers, including other species of dragonfly.

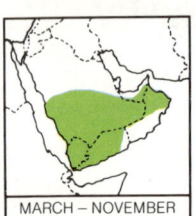
MARCH – NOVEMBER

***Trithemis kirbyi* Sélys**   (Orange Darter).   The body and the 2 wing patches are bright orange. Not found in oases, but inhabits boulder-strewn wadis in which water is found. It perches on top of the hot rocks with abdomen pointing vertically up, a characteristic habit of all *Crocothemis* and *Trithemis* species.

MAY – NOVEMBER

***Trithemis arteriosa* Burmeister** (Gulley Darter)   This migratory species is more cosmopolitan than *T. kirbyi* (Orange Darter), but shares a preference for hot rocky gullies leading off major wadis. Males and females seldom fly together; males prefer large areas of water on wadi floor, whereas females generally frequent rock faces from which small trickles of water emanate. Apart from colour difference between male and female, the species varies in colour according to locality. In central Saudi Arabia, the colour of wing patches is very faint. The specimen illustrated is from northern Oman.

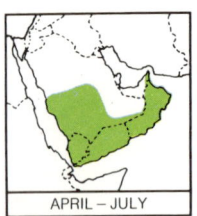
APRIL – JULY

***Pantala flavescens* Fabricius** (Globe Skimmer)   A large species, often seen hawking for insects over sizable pools in wadis of the Tuwayq Hills. Devours prey while flying. Behaviour similar to Aeshnidae family (Hawker Dragonflies). It is a very strong flier, which may account for its widespread distribution. Found in many parts of the world and may only be a migrant to Saudi Arabia.

MARCH – NOVEMBER

***Selysiothemis nigra* van der Linden** (Desert Darter)   Common in oases, it migrates during March and April. Adult males are sometimes almost as dark as *Diplacodes lefebvrei* (Purple Darter), but wing venation is always much lighter in colour. Probably one of the most widespread dragonflies in Eastern Arabia. (See p. 7 for illustration of adult.)

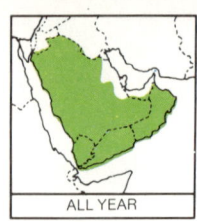

ALL YEAR

Crocothemis erythraea **Brullé** (Carmine Darter)   The most widespread dragonfly in Saudi Arabia. Male is a bright carmine red, in distinct contrast to the yellow and buff of the female and immature insect. It prefers a habitat of rocky watercourses, desert pools and barren irrigation channels, but avoids oases.

A

ALL YEAR

Crocothemis chaldaeorum **Morton** (Scarlet Darter)   Some authorities consider this to be a subspecies of *C. erythraea* (Carmine Darter), but its ecology is quite distinct. In Saudi Arabia, at least, it prefers oasis pools with reeds or rivers with reeds and is never found elsewhere except during its northerly migrations in April. Even in regions where the two species occupy the same general area (such as Al Hasa oasis), *C. chaldaeorum* is always found within the oasis and *C. erythraea* outside the oasis. The two populations never mix. It would appear that *C. chaldaeorum* has evolved in the oases of eastern Saudi Arabia and since the last ice age spread north and east to Iraq and Qatar. Slightly smaller and darker than *C. erythraea*.   **B**

Orthoptera or Saltatoria
(Crickets and Grasshoppers)

The majority of insects in this order have very large hindlegs, used for leaping. Many entomologists consider that the alternative name, Saltatoria, is more appropriate, since this is derived from the Latin word *saltare*, to leap. All insects within the order have a large pronotum, which is a hard casing in the form of a saddle situated behind the head. It acts as a protection to the prothorax and in certain species it is extended to cover the whole of the abdomen. Some species have 2 pairs of wings, others have none. For those that have wings, the front pair are narrow and made of a tough leathery cuticle. These act as a protection to encase the more delicate hindwings which are used in flight. Apart from locusts, the Saltatoria are poor fliers and rely on their large hindlegs to obtain power-assisted gliding. Consequently, wide expanses of water generally act as a barrier to the distribution of insects belonging to this order.

The sexes can be distinguished by the shape of the rear end of the abdomen. The body of the female cricket has an ovipositor at its extremity, whereas the body of the male is lacking in this appendage. The body of the female grasshopper is horizontal at its extremity, whereas the body of the male turns up. All species have compound eyes and in addition may have 2 or 3 ocelli. Most species are vegetarian and generally feed on grass, but some do eat small insects; after mating, some females have been observed to devour the male. The eggs are laid underground and the development includes an incomplete metamorphosis.

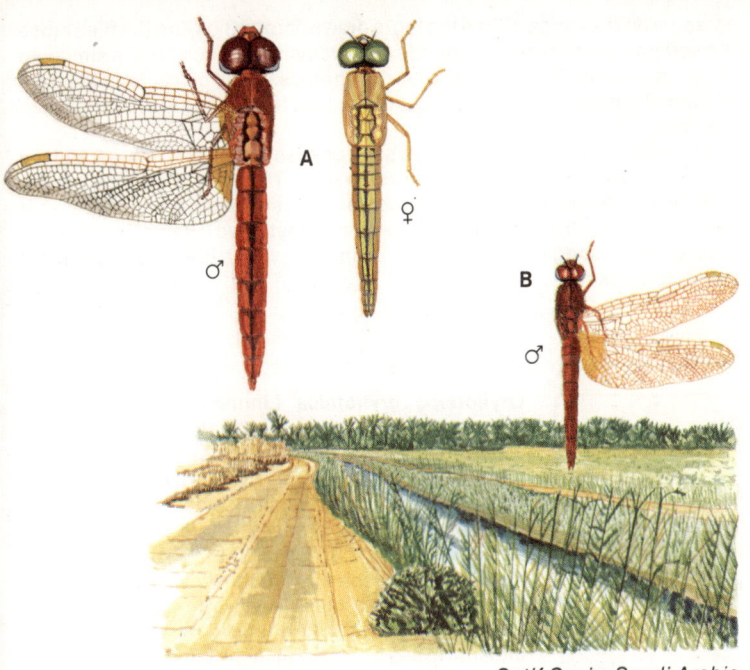

Qatif Oasis, Saudi Arabia

The young insects look like small adults and undergo between 5 and 8 moults. For some species, wing buds form during the last few moults and the wings become complete after the last moult.

The insects in the order fall into five main types:

Mole Crickets
Crickets
Bush Crickets (long antennae)
Ground Hoppers
Short Horned Grasshoppers (short antennae)

All species have hearing devices and members of each species are capable of communicating by sound. Generally they will not 'sing' until the air temperature has reached an acceptable level. The hearing device or tympanic organ for a cricket is situated in the forelegs, that for grasshoppers at the base of the abdomen. The sound is produced by vibrating the forewing. Crickets have protrusions (files) on the right wing and ridged veins (scrapers) on the left wing, which produce the stridulations when rubbed together. Only the male cricket can produce stridulation and his song is a continuous one. The sound is considered to be attractive and in some European countries field crickets are kept in small cages as pets. Grasshoppers have files on the legs and scrapers on the wings. When the leg is drawn across the wing the files cross the scrapers and a series of sounds (or stridulation) occur. This is similar to the sound produced when a pencil is drawn across a hair comb. Both the male and female grasshopper can sing, although the female has less volume than the male.

Grasshoppers can have one fixed song or a number of fixed songs, and the solo song is different from the courtship song. The volume and pitch is different for each species and only members of that species are receptive to that particular song. In some instances, entomologists find it easier to identify a species by its song than by visual examination, which is especially true for the Mole Crickets.

Gryllotalpidae (Mole Crickets)

ALL YEAR

***Gryllotalpa gryllotalpa* Linnaeus** (Mole Cricket)
The front legs are very powerful and fitted with claws which enable it to excavate tunnels in soft soil. Spends much of its life underground, where it lives on a diet of various plant roots and small insects; favoured habitat is cultivated fields in oases. There is a similar but smaller species, *G. africana*. Both species can fly and stridulate. They form part of the diet of the Hoopoe, a striking bird with black and white barred wings, a crested pink head and a long curved bill. It is not unusual to see a number of these birds systematically work their way across a field, clearing it of subterranean insects. Female Mole Crickets do not possess an external ovipositor and lay their eggs in underground chambers which they guard. They tend the young for the first few weeks.

Gryllidae (True Crickets)

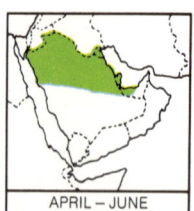
APRIL – JUNE

***Acheta domestica* Linnaeus** (House Cricket)
Native to Arabia. Seldom seen due to its nocturnal lifestyle, but may be exposed when stones or sacking are turned over. It has spread throughout Europe by exploiting warm environments provided by human habitation, for example rubbish tips, which gain their heat from rotting vegetable refuse, or in bakehouses. Can be of considerable annoyance to inhabitants of a house due to the continual nocturnal chirruping, but causes little harm since it lives off small scraps of waste food and rubbish.

Qurum, Northern Oman

MARCH – OCTOBER

Gryllus bimaculatus de Geer (Tropical Field Cricket)
Although unable to fly and only able to make small jumps, this is probably the most common cricket in Arabia, as it is found in most gardens and oases. Capable of producing one of the loudest insect songs in Arabia. A ground dweller with nocturnal habits.

Tettigoniidae (Bush Crickets)

Members of this family are sometimes called Long Horned Grasshoppers because they possess very long antennae; however, they are closely related to Crickets.

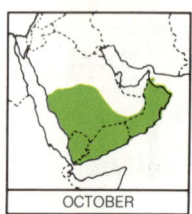
OCTOBER

***Phaneroptera sparsa* Stål** (Pale Bush Cricket) Generally common among lush vegetation, where this occurs within its range. Can fly and jump, but prefers to walk. Female has very large ovipositor which looks dangerous although the insect is harmless.

Acrididae (Grasshoppers)

This family is often referred to as Short-Horned Grasshoppers since all the species included have short antennae.

FEBRUARY – AUGUST

***Anacridium aegyptium* Linnaeus** (Egyptian Tree-Locust) With a similar species, *A.melanorhodon*, (not included in this book) it frequents trees in oases and gardens where sometimes it can be found in large numbers. Has been known to defoliate individual trees, but unlike true locusts does not form swarms. A good flier and generally, when disturbed, makes short swift flights between trees or bushes.

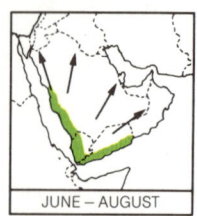
JUNE – AUGUST

***Locusta migratoria* Linnaeus** (Migratory Locust) Occurs in small numbers throughout Arabia, but rarely forms into swarms. Has 2 colour forms, brown and green. Specimen illustrated is an adult female, solitary phase (or green form). Under favourable breeding conditions, millions of young 'hoppers' will congregate and march in a given direction. As they grow into adulthood they undergo a change, but the green pigment so prevalent in the solitary adult does not develop, and the shape of the body also differs from the solitary adult. Gregarious adults may all take off in a swarm. They are very strong fliers and migratory specimens have been recorded from Central Europe and Britain.

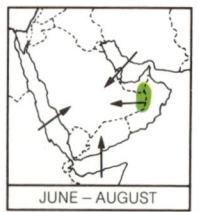
JUNE – AUGUST

***Schistocerca gregaria* Forskål** (Desert Locust) In Arabia it forms swarms more readily than *Locusta migratoria* (Migratory Locust). Enormous swarms sometimes occur in western Saudi Arabia and northern Oman, but are usually restricted to these areas. (Not illustrated.)

Eruca vesicaria (Rocket)

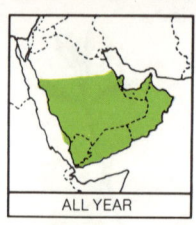
ALL YEAR

***Truxalis procera* Klug** (Gangling Grasshopper) A number of similar *Truxalis* species occur in Arabia, but *T. procera* is the most common and widespread. It inhabits the fringes of oases and grassy hollows in open desert. In drier areas it tends to be less green, and in some localities completely brown forms occur. Flight is short but fast, just above the vegetation.

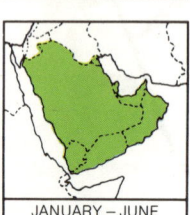
JANUARY – JUNE

***Aiolopus thalassinus* Fabricius** (Grass Pest) Has 2 colour forms, green and brown, both illustrated. Main food is grass and the insect is common wherever this grows. The green form is predominant in oases where the colour acts as a good camouflage among the more lush vegetation. During recent years it has become a pest on many farms in central Saudi Arabia and Oman where grass is grown for fodder.

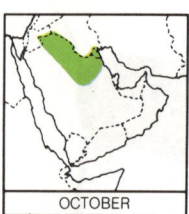
OCTOBER

***Ochrilidia gracilis* Krauss** (Pale Slant Face) A number of *Ochrilidia* species occur in Arabia, but all look very similar to *O. gracilis*. It inhabits areas of luxuriant grass in farms and oases, where it can often be found in good numbers.

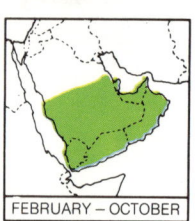
FEBRUARY – OCTOBER

***Pyrgomorpha conica* Olivier** (Hollow Grasshopper) Found where grass grows in oases, farms, wadis and gardens, it is widespread and generally numerous. Another closely related species, *P. cognata* (not included in this book), has similar habits and is also found in the same localities, but is less common. The two insects are so similar they can only be distinguished by dissection. They also both vary in colour and size according to locality.

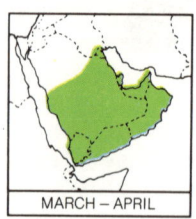
MARCH – APRIL

***Morphacris fasciata* Thunberg** (Sooty Cheek) Found in similar habitats to those frequented by *Pyrgomorpha conica* (Hollow Grasshopper). Inspection of the head confirms identification. Both cheeks are shiny black, each with a cream-coloured 'comma' mark; also, the entire head is covered with backward sloping lines.

Haplophyllum tuberculatum (Desert Rue)

FEBRUARY – JUNE

***Heteracris littoralis* Rambur** (Yellow Streak) Similar to another species, *H. annulosus* (not included in this book), they differ only in the number of spines on hindlegs. Both species inhabit stony fringes of oases, rocky hollows and desert farms where they live on low vegetation and bushes. In proportion to their size these insects are capable of jumping higher than any other Arabian insect.

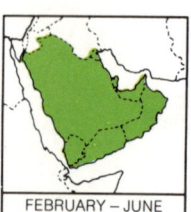
FEBRUARY – JUNE

***Sphingonotus rubescens* Walker** (Blue Shinned Grasshopper) A true desert species, generally found during summer wherever grass is growing. When disturbed, it jumps up with noisy wings, flies a few metres and lands on the desert floor. Due to superb camouflage it is almost impossible to discern where it has landed. Tibia is a pale blue.

MAY

***Pseudosphingonotus savignyi* Saussure** (Banded Cloak) A rare species, it occupies the same terrain as *Sphingonotus rubescens* (Blue Shinned Grasshopper). Makes more noise in flight than the latter.

JANUARY – MAY

***Poekilocerus bufonius* Klug** (Milkweed Toadi) One of the most striking insects in Arabia. Its bright colours warn potential predators that it is poisonous. Derives the poison from foodplants, *Pergularia* and *Calotropis*. Because of this defence it makes very little effort to escape when approached. If attacked, will first flash its vivid red hindwings as an additional warning. If attacker persists, the grasshopper will envelop itself in a foul-tasting, frothy liquid secreted from its abdomen. Both male and female are large and often incapable of flying or jumping effectively.

APRIL – JULY

***Utubius syriacus* Bolivar** (Syrian Thickthigh) This uncommon species frequents stony deserts strewn with *Rhanterium* plants. Mainly an insect of the Levant; Saudi Arabia is the southernmost limit of its range. It is large and a poor jumper, but can fly well. Colour of the hindwings is green and black, but when at rest the insect relies on excellent camouflage to avoid detection.

Tetrigidae (Ground Hoppers)

A primitive group. Ground hoppers are unable to produce sound and do not possess hearing organs (ears). Due to their small size and dull coloration they are seldom seen, but are common on sparsely vegetated ground near water.

MARCH – OCTOBER

***Hedotettix alienus* Uvarov** (Swamp Hopper) This species is strictly confined to edges of shallow freshwater pools in oases, but is not common.

JULY – AUGUST

***Paratettix ocellatus* Uvarov** (Gravel Hopper) To date it has only been recorded from northern Oman, but probably exists in parts of Saudi Arabia. Inhabits rock-strewn riverbeds in mountainous areas where it often congregates in large numbers on gravel bars. When disturbed it generally leaps into the water to escape and is capable of swimming well. Looks very similar to *Hedotettix alienus* (Swamp Hopper). To distinguish the species it is best to view the insect head-on. *P. ocellatus* has a dip between the eyes, whereas *H. alienus* has a ridge.

Wadi Shaib Luha, Riyadh, Saudi Arabia

Dermaptera
(Earwigs)

All insects of this small order possess a strong pair of curved pincers at the end of the abdomen which have evolved from a modification of the cerci. When threatened the abdomen is curved upwards to display these pincers. The insects have compound eyes but no ocelli. The antennae are composed of a large number of segments which are very sensitive and used constantly to explore the surroundings. The front wings are small, hard and meet in the middle like the elytra of beetles. The hindwings are large, membranous and have the texture of human skin, giving rise to the scientific name Dermaptera. Each hindwing, when open, has the shape of a quadrant of a circle and has to be folded a great number of times to be housed under the front wings. The insect has been observed to use its pincers to assist in folding the wings. The sexes can be easily identified; female pincers are short and narrow, whereas those of the male are larger and more curved.

Despite their fierce appearance earwigs are shy and inoffensive. They are nocturnal and rest during the day beneath stones, behind bark or among debris. At night they scavenge for plant material, small insects, carrion and fungi. They are harmless to man, but their secretive habits have on occasions tempted them to investigate the ears of sleeping people, which may have given rise to the name earwig. Although a primitive order, the insects demonstrate very advanced behaviour in caring for their young. Eggs laid in the soil are tended by the female throughout the winter. When they hatch she feeds and tends the young until they are able to fend for themselves.

Labiduridae (Long-tailed Earwigs)

JANUARY – MAY

***Labidura riparia* Pallas** (Tawny or Shore Earwig) The largest and most common earwig in Arabia. Found in almost any damp or wet situation, the fringe of irrigated areas being a favourite locality. This species extends across Europe and was found at one locality in England, although it is now thought to be extinct there.

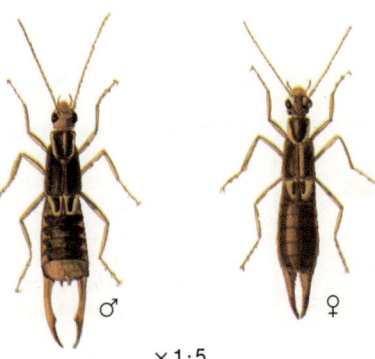

× 1·5

Dictyoptera
(Cockroaches and Mantises)

This is a very primitive order of insect. Fossil remains of cockroaches have been found with fossil dragonflies from the Upper Carboniferous period. The insects that exist today bear a close resemblance to those which lived over 300 million years ago. Mainly denizens of countries with hot climates, cockroaches have spread throughout the world by inhabiting kitchens, bakehouses and other areas which are kept artificially warm. Most species are nocturnal and omnivorous, both features being contributory factors to their survival and success. Cockroaches are generally flat in shape, a characteristic which helps them to hide during the day in cracks and crevices. They feed at night on a variety of foods which include dead animal remains, rotting vegetation, food scraps and even the grease and bacterial films found in drains.

Blattidae (Cockroaches)

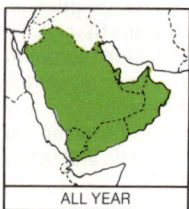
ALL YEAR

***Periplaneta americana* Linnaeus** (American Cockroach) It is not known how this insect obtained its name, as it was originally a native of Africa where it frequented damp animal burrows and caves. Now has a worldwide distribution, although often living under artificial conditions. Found in most buildings in Arabia, where it usually dwells in the drains, but will also forage for food at night. Prefers to run when startled, but can fly and this appears to be the main method of colonising new premises.. **A**

ALL YEAR

***Blatella germanica* Linnaeus** (German Cockroach) The name is misleading because it is not a native of Germany, but originated from North Africa. It is found throughout the world and can occur in very large numbers under favourable conditions. Frequents damp, dark areas in kitchens and bathrooms and other buildings, where it may live behind loose panelling or beneath the floors. The female practises a primitive form of maternal care and carries the oothecae until shortly before the eggs hatch. **B**

APRIL – NOVEMBER

***Blatella mellea* Krauss** (Eremic Cockroach) Although closely related to *B. germanica* (German Cockroach), it has been unable to take advantage of the opportunities offered by human activity. It is restricted to the Middle East, and is found in most oases and gardens living amongst vegetation, especially grass. Nymphs are often very common, and distinguished from adults by 2 dark bands on the pronutum and by a lack of wings. **C**

These insects have a large pronotum which covers most of the head, very long sensitive antennae, long spiky legs and cerci. Most species have 2 pairs of wings: the front pair are leathery and are folded flat over the body when not in use; the hindwings are membranous and have a great number of veins. The insects are hypersensitive to disturbance and can fly, but generally disappear very quickly by running. Many are considered pests because they can contaminate food with disease germs. The food may also be tainted by a characteristic unpleasant odour. Eggs are laid in purses called oothecae which are generally deposited in a crack or crevice. Some species carry the oothecae around until shortly before the eggs are due to hatch. Young cockroaches are called nymphs and look similar to the adults.

Mantises have several characteristics which are similar to cockroaches. Most species inhabit countries with hot climates and the females also lay eggs in an ootheca. The insect has a large pronotum, but it does not cover the head. The front wings are leathery and fold flat with an overlap. The hindwings are large, membranous, often colourful and concertina under the front wings when not in use. A mantis is a fierce predator which likes to eat prey alive. It usually feeds on insects, but will occasionally eat small lizards. It relies on camouflage until an unsuspecting creature comes within reach, before lunging with its front legs and grasping the victim which is then drawn back to the mouth and eaten alive. The front legs are armed with spikes and have 2 joints, which enables them to be held folded in front of the body and gives rise to the name Praying Mantis.

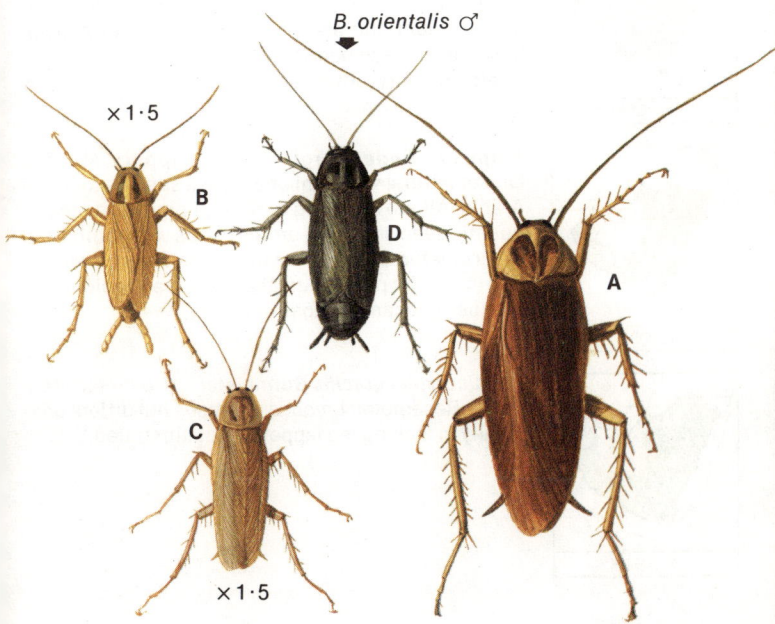

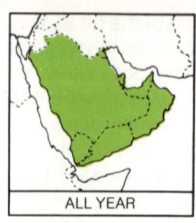
ALL YEAR

***Blatta orientalis* Linnaeus** (Common Cockroach) Sometimes referred to as the 'Black Beetle', it frequents damp stores and cellars, but is not common in Arabia as it prefers more temperate zones. Female carries the oothecae for some time after laying eggs. The female cannot fly, and the male flies with difficulty because of its small wings. However, both can run very fast. (See p. 25, fig. D.)

APRIL – JUNE

***Blatta lateralis* Walker** (Dimorphic Cockroach) A native of Arabia, where it frequents damp hollows, wadis and desert farms. Very little association with man; spends most of the day beneath stones and feeds at night. Females cannot fly, and differ in colour and size from male. Both sexes illustrated.

Mantidae (Praying Mantises)

JULY – NOVEMBER

***Blepharopsis mendica* Fabricius** (Striped Mantis) Although boldly marked with bright green and white stripes, it is extremely difficult to detect among low vegetation. Favourite plants are *Haloxylon* and *Zygophyllum*, but also frequents stands of *Acacia*. Males are more slender than females and have very pectinate (feathery) antennae. **A**

OCTOBER

***Empusa hedenborgi* Stål** (Lappet Mantis) One of several very similar *Empusa* species found in Arabia. All are attracted to light at night and are frequently seen scurrying around walls with moths and other creatures. During the day they sit among vegetation in wait for prey, where their shape and colour provide perfect camouflage. **B**

OCTOBER

***Hypsicorypha gracilis* Burmeister** (Helmeted Mantis) Resembles *Empusa* mantises but differs principally in lacking leg lappets. (Not illustrated.)

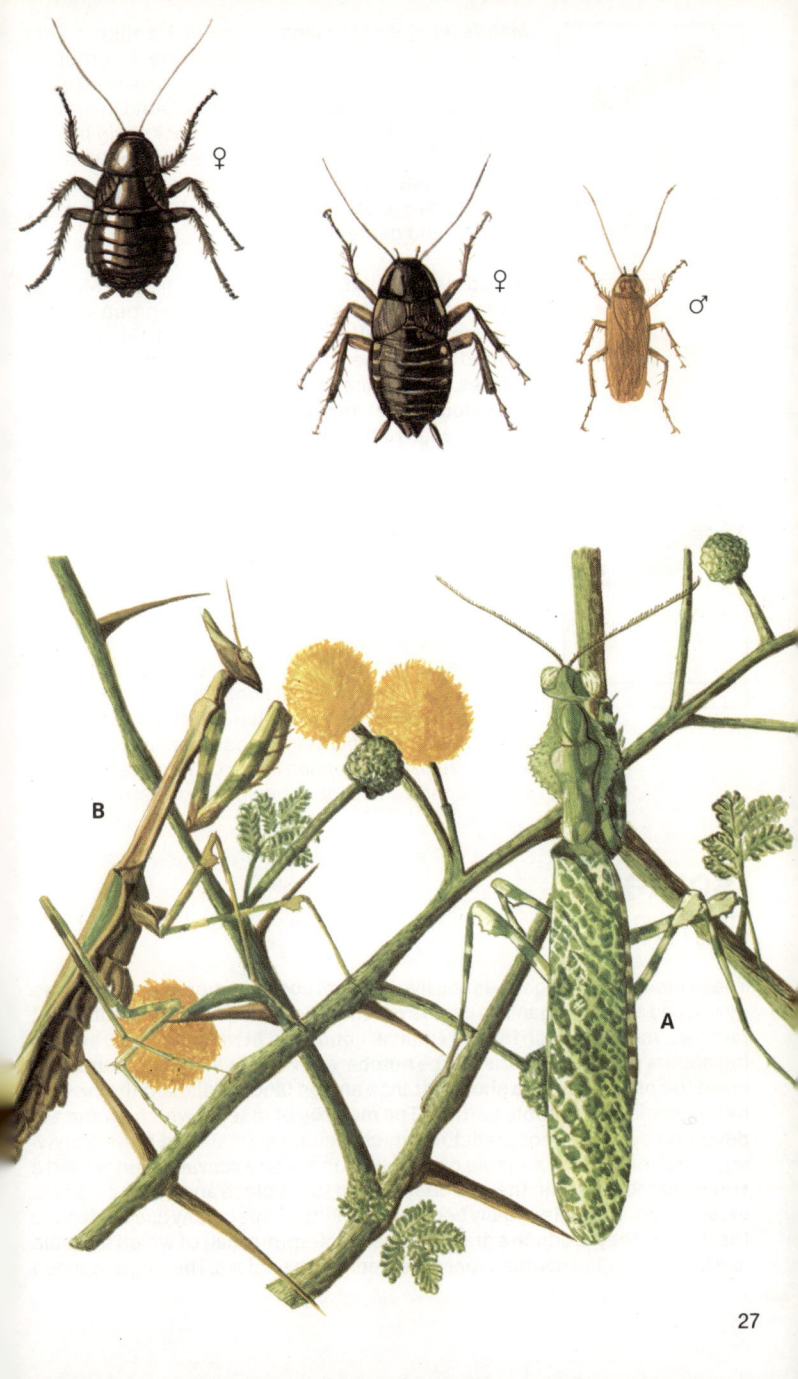

JULY – NOVEMBER

***Mantis religiosa* Linnaeus** (Praying Mantis) First described by Linnaeus, this insect gave the group its common name. Mainly an insect of the Levant, Mediterranean and Central Europe, it is only found in the northern part of the Arabian Peninsula. Lacks twig-like appearance of *Empusa* mantises and is of a more uniform shape. Consequently, it is poorly camouflaged among true desert vegetation and prefers leafier surroundings of oases and gardens.

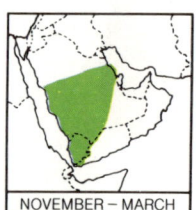
NOVEMBER – MARCH

***Oxyothespis nilotica* Giglio-Tos** (Fairy Mantis) There are several similar species in this group and it is extremely difficult to identify them individually. It is beyond the scope of this book to name individual species, but a typical species is illustrated. Their shape and colour render them almost invisible when situated among twigs of their herbaceous habitat.

MARCH – APRIL

***Eremiaphila braueri* Krauss** (Common Ground Mantis) Most mantises dwell in trees and shrubs, but the various species of the genus *Eremiaphila* are found on stony ground. Their general shape and colour resemble a small pebble. Unless they move, this camouflage defies detection even with the closest scrutiny. They are also elusive in motion as their speed is so fast and sudden, especially in bright sunlight when it is easy to question whether they were there at all. As they rely on their speed and camouflage, most species are without wings. *Eremiaphila braueri* is one of the more common species and can be identified by black barred wings.

Isoptera
(Termites)

These insects are gregarious and live in social communities where they have developed a highly organized caste system. The order contains many different families, most of which inhabit tropical countries. In most species, swarming occurs periodically when large numbers of winged adults of both sexes leave the nest. They fly a short distance and on landing discard their wings before seeking a suitable partner. The majority of insects which swarm are devoured by a variety of predators which include animals and birds. Surviving pairs search for a suitable place where they can excavate a tunnel and a small chamber. Within the chamber mating takes place and a new colony is established. The male usually becomes the king of this colony and the female the queen. They produce a great number of offspring, half of which are male and half female, but normally these are sterile and wingless. The king and queen

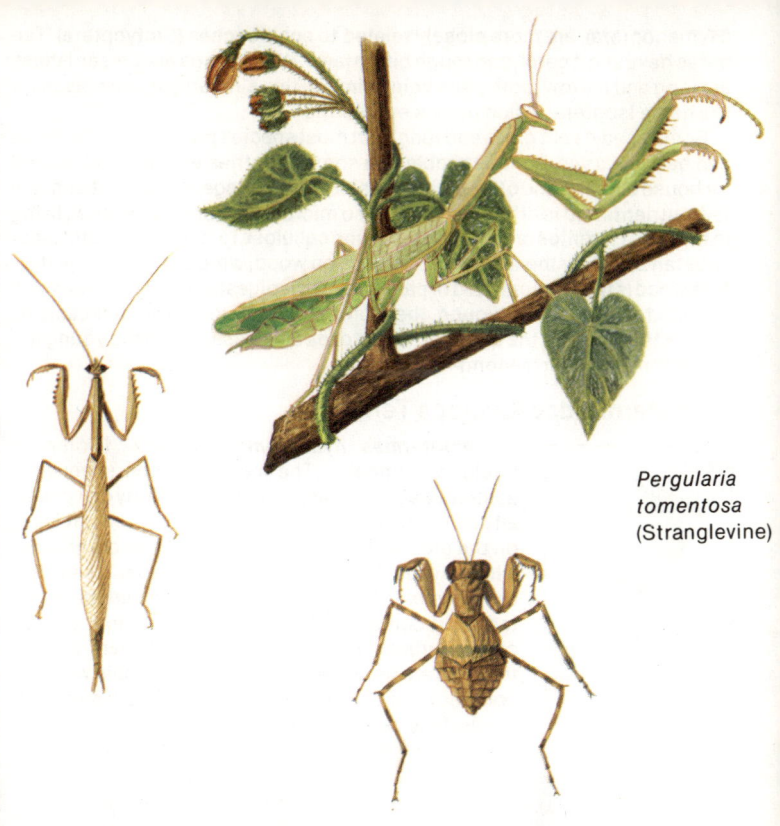

Pergularia tomentosa (Stranglevine)

mate periodically and have been known to live together for 50 years, producing a colony that can number many millions.

Termites are classed as exopterygote insects because they have neither a larval nor a pupal stage in their growth. However, several different castes occur which differ considerably in appearance. The worker caste is the most numerous and is composed of juvenile insects of various ages which often never mature. These can change into soldiers or reproductive forms if necessary. Of the two types of soldier termites which occur, one has very large and formidable jaws, whereas the other has a pear-shaped head with glands from which a repellent liquid can be ejected against attackers. If the king and queen are destroyed, some colonies can produce a supplementary reproductive caste to replace them. Termites, although superficially resembling ants

(Hymenoptera), are more closely related to cockroaches (Dictyoptera). Termites have short cerci, and tough biting jaws. When wings are present these are long and narrow, both pairs being similar; this similarity is the reason for the name Isoptera, which means equal wings.

Some species eat grass and fungi, but most species prefer wood. Termites can become a very serious problem in some countries where wood is used for house building and often cause considerable damage. Wood contains very few nutrients and is difficult to digest, so micro-organisms (protozoa), living in the gut of termites break down the tough cellulose to form sugars and other substances. Only the worker caste feeds on wood, which is partly digested. This wood is then regurgitated or passed as partly digested faecal pellets which are used as food for the young, the reproductive caste, the soldier caste as well as the king and the queen. The protozoa are passed on to the young termites through their 'second-hand' food.

Rhinotermitidae (Cyclops Termites)

MARCH – APRIL

***Psammotermes hybostoma* Desneux** (Common Cyclops Termite)   The most common species in eastern Arabia. In damp locations a colony can generally be found under any large piece of wood left lying on the ground. Most of the nest will be underground, with only the feeding galleries in the wood itself. The caste system of this species differs from the typical pattern as it contains both a major and a minor soldier caste. During March and April numerous dark-winged termites are produced, which under suitable weather conditions of thunder and strong thermals swarm to the surface and take flight.

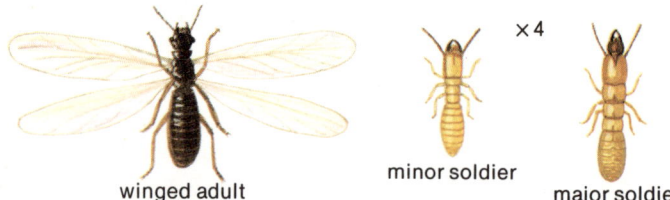

winged adult   minor soldier   ×4   major soldier

Psocoptera and Mallophaga
(Booklice and Biting Lice)

Psocoptera (Booklice) includes a number of small insects with soft bodies that feed on a variety of stored items. They often inhabit libraries and museums. Little is known of their habits in Arabia and they are not included in this text. Insects of the order Mallophaga (Biting Lice) are small and wingless. Most of the species have adapted their shape and habits so that they can survive as parasites on birds, feeding on small pieces of skin or feathers which they bite off their host. A detailed description of species is beyond the scope of this book.

Anoplura
(Sucking Lice)

There are a number of species of Anoplura in Arabia, all with similar habits, which live on mammals, including 2 universal races that live on man. Their legs have claws which permit the louse to retain a very firm grip on the hairs of the victim. The mouths of these lice are adapted to pierce and suck blood, but can be retracted into the body when not in use. Most species are blind and avoid light. The breathing organs are on the upper surface of the insect.

Pediculidae

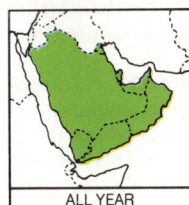
ALL YEAR

***Pediculus humanus capitis* de Geer** (Human Head Louse)

× 5

ALL YEAR

***Pediculus humanus humanus* Linnaeus** (Human Body Louse)
There are two separate races of this louse, which limit their activities to different parts of the human form. *Pediculus capitis* (Head Louse) is more prevalent in children and lives in hair on the head where it lays its eggs. The eggs are known as nits. *Pediculus humanus* (Body Louse) lives on body hairs and usually lays its eggs in adjacent clothing. The eggs generally hatch in 1 week. Larvae look similar to adults and take a further 2 weeks to mature. The mature louse is grey, but the immature louse will assume the colour of the victim, pale insects being found on blond hair and dark insects on black hair. When feeding, it may take on a rosy colour as it becomes gorged with blood. Saliva produced while feeding causes a lot of irritation to the victim and induces scratching. The resulting wounds may become infected with germs. The Head Louse is not known to carry dangerous germs, but the Body Louse can transmit *Typhus* and other serious illnesses. Lice are easily eradicated with proper medication, good hygiene and clean clothes.

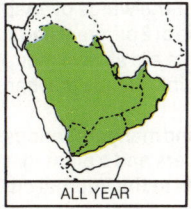
ALL YEAR

***Phthirus pubis* Linnaeus** (Crab Louse) A rare parasite on man. It lives and lays eggs in the hairs of the pubic region. It is shaped like a small crab and is light grey or purple. Not known to carry serious diseases.

Hemiptera
(True Bugs, Cicadas, Plant Hoppers and Aphids)

This order contains a large number of insects which differ greatly in size, colour, shape and habits. They belong to many different families which at first sight appear to be unrelated. However, they have one common characteristic — their food is sucked in liquid form from a live host. All the insects have a rostrum, the name given to a stiff proboscis. This acts like a syringe and is capable of piercing the skin of the host and withdrawing liquids. The majority of the species attack plants and feed off sap, but some species feed off the blood of animals and insects. Among the latter is *Cimex lectularius* (Bed Bug) which feeds off man.

The antennae of the Hemiptera are often long in comparison to the size of the insect, but comprise only a few segments, usually 4 or 5 and seldom more than 10. The insects do not possess cerci and some species lack wings. Those that have wings fold them with an overlap when not in use. This helps to distinguish the order from beetles whose front wings (elytra) meet along the centre line of the body.

During evolution the Hemiptera adapted 4 organs — the mandibles, maxillae, labium and labrum — to form the rostrum. These organs work in conjunction with one another to provide the efficient system that extracts liquid food from the host. The labium forms an outer sheath to the rostrum which contains 2 pairs of stylets and 2 channels. When feeding commences, the rostrum is placed in contact with the skin of the plant or animal. As it is forced down, the labium buckles to expose the stylets, which pierce the skin and penetrate to the food source. Saliva is pumped down one of the channels to act as an anticoagulant. In some bugs the saliva is poisonous and may kill the host. Diluted food is sucked up the second channel. When not in use the rostrum is generally held horizontally under the body.

The order Hemiptera is divided into two distinct suborders: the Heteroptera and the Homoptera. The Heteroptera contains a great variety of different insects many of which feed off plants, although some feed off mammals and others off insects. The suborder also contains all of the bugs that live in or on fresh water.

They generally have flat bodies, are often brightly coloured and have compound eyes and usually two ocelli, with the exception of the water bugs which have no ocelli. The rostrum is at the front of the head and in front of the eyes. Not all species have wings, but when present and at rest the wings overlap and are folded flat over the body. Each front wing is made up of 2 different parts, a hard leathery base and a veined clear tip. The hindwings are always membranous. Some species are poisonous and some have 'stink' glands that can emit an obnoxious liquid.

All species in the suborder Homoptera feed off plants and many are serious pests. These insects generally occur in very large numbers and a plant that is attacked will suffer from loss of sap and from ruptures in the internal circulation system. Toxins contained in the saliva of some species destroy chlorophyll which causes the leaves to turn brown and wither. A more serious threat to agriculture are virus infections transmitted by the insects. Sap, which is the food source, contains a small proportion of protein and a large proportion of sugar. The insects assimilate what they require and any excess, which is mainly sugar, is excreted. This is known generally as honeydew and is very attractive to other insects, particularly ants. Some ants even encourage aphids to discharge honeydew by stroking them with their antennae. The by-product of one of the species has been used by The Bedouin as food and this may have been the food known as 'manna'. Some of the insects also exude a wax as a protection against dessication or predation. The wax from certain insects is collected by man to produce shellac, a high gloss varnish used to polish furniture.

Not all of the Homoptera species have wings, but when wings are present the front pair are of a uniform structure while the hind pair are membranous. At rest, they are folded above the body like a ridge tent. The rostrum is situated beneath the back of the head, the eyes are at the front. Most species have compound eyes and many have 2 or 3 additional ocelli. The Homoptera are divided into 2 distinct divisions which can be differentiated by the antennae. Those that have short, spiky antennae belong to the Auchenorrhyncha (Cicadas and Plant Hoppers) and those with long, thin antennae belong to the Sternorrhyncha (Aphids). The female Cicadas and Plant Hoppers generally have an ovipositor which they use to insert eggs in crevices or within the cells of a plant. Aphids lack an ovipositor but they can be parthenogenetic, which means that they can reproduce from unfertilized eggs. They may also be viviparous, i.e. capable of producing live young. Consequently, they are able to produce large populations very quickly.

Heteroptera (True Bugs)

Miridae (Capsid Bugs)

JANUARY

***Deraeocoris pallens* Reuter** (Check Capsid) Most of the insects in this family live among vegetation and feed upon the sap, seed or fruit of various trees and plants. *Deraeocoris pallens* lives in flower heads, where it preys on small insects that have come in search of nectar.

× 1·5

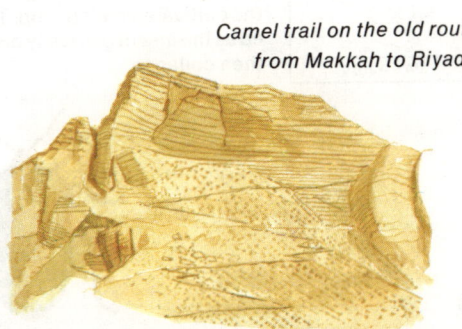

Camel trail on the old route from Makkah to Riyadh

Cydnidae (Soil Bugs)

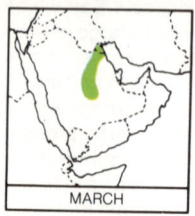
MARCH

***Macroscytus brunneus* Fabricius** (Brown Trog) Most of the year is spent in hibernation below ground, while for the rest of the time it lives among leaf litter and short vegetation. Feeds on short vegetation.

Pentatomidae (Shield Bugs)

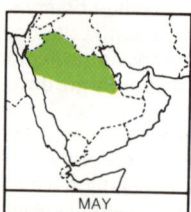
MAY

***Nezara viridula* Linnaeus** (Green Plant Bug) Most members of this family can produce very unpleasant smells, which often taint their food source. *Nezara viridula* has become a minor pest on fruit and vegetables grown in farms and oases. However, its large size and open behaviour make it easy to detect.

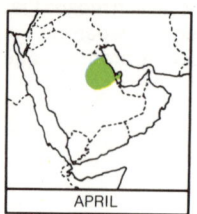
APRIL

***Eysarcoris inconspicuus* Herrich-Schäffer** (Herbage Bug)

Dinidoridae (Melon Bugs)

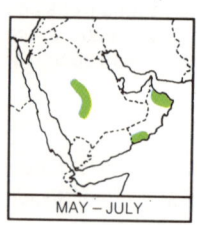
MAY – JULY

***Coridius viduatus* Fabricius** (Melon Bug) Causes major damage to melon crops in Saudi Arabia. At first it confines its attention to wild members of the melon family, such as *Citrullus*. However, as summer approaches, these plants dry up and it then transfers to the cultivated melon crop. The fruit is seldom attacked as the insect generally pierces young stems, which then collapse.

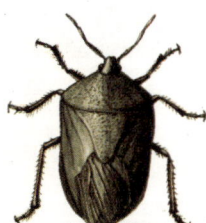

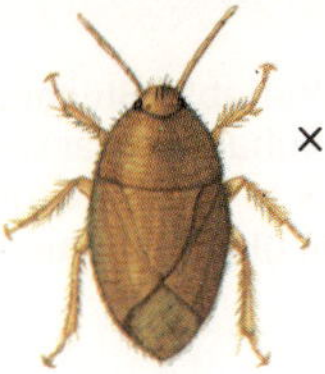

Medicago sativa (Alfalfa)

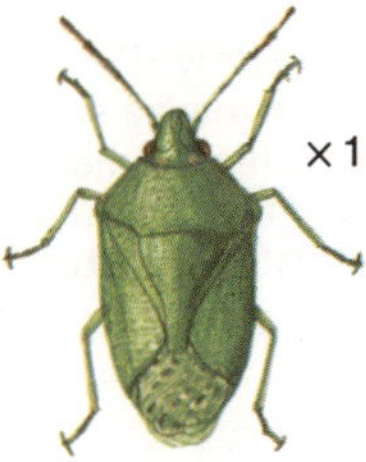

Cimicidae (Bed Bugs)

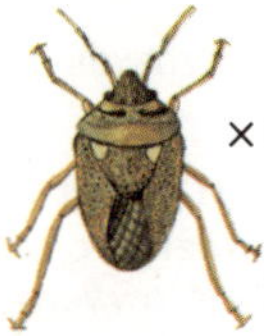

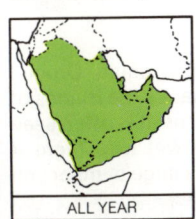

ALL YEAR

***Cimex lectularius* Linnaeus** (Bed Bug) Found throughout most of the world it feeds mainly on man, is nocturnal and hides in clothes and crevices during the day. Its saliva contains an anticoagulant which prevents the host's blood from clotting and also dilutes it to assist the flow up the rostrum. The habits of bed bugs have been known to man for a long time and have not always been considered unwelcome. The ancient Greeks refer to potions which contained the insect. Although the wounds may cause irritation, the insect does not transmit disease. Method of mating is unusual. The male organ pierces the skin of the female permitting sperm to swim through the blood of the female to the eggs. Eggs are laid in clothing and crevices and do not normally hatch unless a person is in the vicinity.

Rhopalidae (Blushing Bugs)

APRIL – MAY

***Liorhyssus hyalinus* Fabricius** (Variable Blushing Bug) A common insect which inhabits grasses. Varies in colour, ranging from pink to brown. Other typical characteristics are its stink gland and membranous front wings.
A

Alydidae (Racer Bugs)

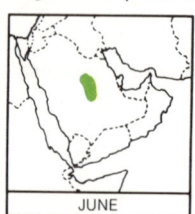

JUNE

***Mirperus jaculus* Thunberg** (Yellow Dagger) Found wherever vegetation occurs, it moves swiftly across the ground but readily takes to flight if disturbed. Nymph lacks wings, but gains some protection by mimicking the dark *Cataglyphis* ants with which it often associates.
B

Lygaeidae (Ground Bugs)

A number of species of Lygaeidae are found in eastern Arabia. They have similar habits and feed off plants in low vegetation.

MARCH

***Dieuches mucronatus* Stål** (Bleached Ground Bug) This species is widespread in Arabia where it can be found running over sandy gravel amongst low vegetation. It rarely flies, like most members of this family.
C

NOVEMBER – JANUARY

***Lygaeus equestris* Linnaeus** (Harlequin Ground Bug) Common in Arabia, it inhabits the fringes of oases and fertile desert depressions. It is often seen running across the ground, but will take flight if threatened. It can be found in very large numbers on *Calotropis procera* (Sodom's Apple).

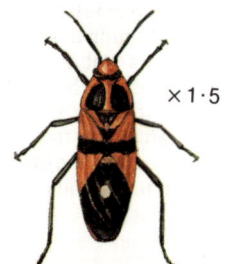

× 1·5

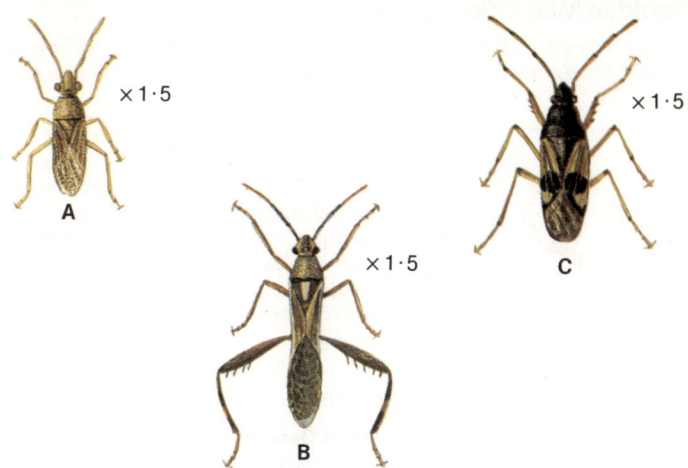

The old fort, Mubarraz, the twin city of Hofuf, Eastern Saudi Arabia

Naucoridae (Saucer Bugs)

Heleocoris minusculus **Walker** (Small Saucer Bug)   This aquatic species, is a predator on other small aquatic insects. Forelegs face forward and are adapted to grasp prey. To breathe under water it takes a bubble of air with it when submerging. When natural pools of water dry out during the hot season, it flies to water tanks and other more permanent pools.

37

Nepidae (Water Scorpions)

Nepidae breath by thrusting their long posterior siphon or respiratory tube through the surface of the water. The air collected is stored for future use under the wings.

MARCH – JULY

***Laccotrephes fabricii* Stål** (Stretched Water Scorpion) Although common in mountain streams and pools of western Saudi Arabia, it is a rarity in central Saudi Arabia and absent from the east of the country. It cannot fly and is consequently confined to permanent bodies of water where it lives among submerged vegetation. Not a strong swimmer and generally crawls around in search of prey which it grasps with powerful raptorial forelegs.

Notonectidae (Water Boatmen)

DECEMBER – MARCH

***Anisops debilis* Gerstäcker** (Pigmy Backswimmer) A fierce predator which preys on other insects. Often occurs in large numbers. It is easily identified as it swims on its back using the long, hairy hindlegs as oars. To breathe under water they collect bubbles of air, which are trapped in their ventral hairs and utilised as required. It is also a strong flier which enables it to seek out new ponds when the present habitat becomes untenable.

Homoptera (Cicadas, Plant Hoppers and Aphids)

Cicadidae (Cicadas)

Young cicadas lead a subterranean life and feed upon roots of trees. Their front legs are very sturdy and are used mainly for digging. They spend several years in the nymphal stages and finally emerge from the ground, shedding their immature skins which may be found at the base of trees. One of the skins is illustrated. Wings develop during the last instar. The flight of all cicadas is very fast; after a sudden take off it rises slightly then takes a straight course to the new destination.

APRIL – NOVEMBER

***Platypleura arabica* Myers** (Arabian Cicada) Largest of the Arabian Cicadas, they are very common in Qatar, the United Arab Emirates and Oman where they can be found in most stands of trees. They sit and feed on the smaller branches. Most of the day the male sings, but any local disturbance brings an immediate cessation to his song, which is resumed only when danger has passed. The song produced varies between species, but is always loud and almost continuous. The sound is produced by 2 organs, known as tymbals, situated on either side of the abdomen. The tymbals vibrate rapidly and the sound is magnified by resonance

nymph

within body cavities. Female cannot sing, but is attracted to the rendezvous by the song of males. This results in very large numbers collecting in one area. After mating, female uses her ovipositor to lay eggs.

MAY

***Psalmocharias flavicollis* Horvath**   (Orange Flushed Cicada)   Prefers rocky areas where it frequents *Acacia* trees. Congregates in small numbers. Male sings for short periods only during midsummer.

AUGUST

***Melampsalta musiva* Germar**   (Tiger Cicada)   An insect of low scrub in rocky desert and rarely seen unless disturbed.

Dictyopharidae (Lantern Flies)

General name Plant Hopper includes a number of families with similar habits.

OCTOBER

***Philotheria* spp.**   (Unicorn Hoppers)   Found on a variety of different plants, it leaps into the air when disturbed. Most Unicorn Hoppers may be identified by a forward-projecting head.

Aphididae (Aphids or Plant Lice)

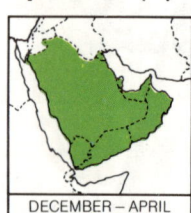

DECEMBER — APRIL

***Myzus persicae* Sulzer**   (Peach and Potato Aphid) A pest of peaches and potatoes in Europe, it also attacks a variety of other plants. In Arabia it principally attacks almonds and radish plants. Although these insects are less than 3 mm in length, damage is caused by heavy infestation with populations which are often in the order of several million. Capable of reproducing rapidly during favourable weather, females can reproduce without mating (parthenogenetically) and produce both wingless and winged forms. Winged forms are able to colonise new areas. To overcome adverse weather conditions, eggs are laid.

×3

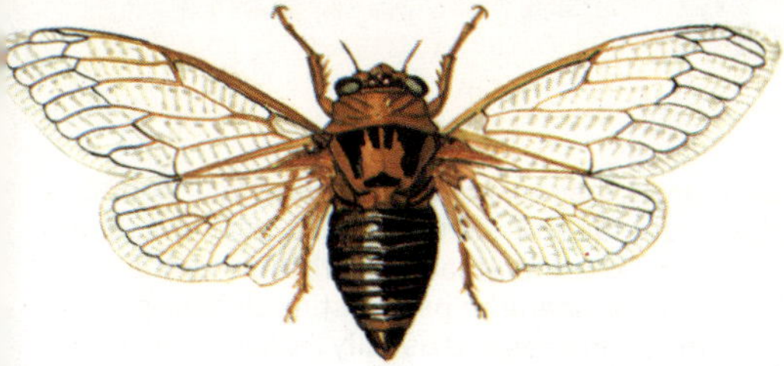

DECEMBER – APRIL

***Aphis nerii* Boyer de Fonscolombe** (Milkweed Aphid) A colourful black and yellow species which generally makes its first appearance as an adult in December, when it can be found on varieties of Milkweed such as *Pergularia tomentosa* (Stranglevine) and *Calotropis procera* (Sodom's Apple). Enormous colonies build up on young shoots among the flowers and under the leaves, although they appear to produce very little damage. During March and April new colonies form on *Nerium oleander* (Oleander) and on *Plumeria* spp. (Frangipani), producing unsightly yellow masses on tender growths resulting in reduced vigour and deformity of the plants.

a colony of wingless forms

Thysanoptera
(Thrips)

Most insects in this order are minute, their average length being approximately 3 mm. They are generally dark in colour, with slender bodies, and have 2 pairs of narrow wings. These are shaped like a bird's feather and have a central spine with fine hairs attached. This unusual shape helps to distinguish thrips from all other orders. They have compound eyes and usually 3 ocelli. The mouth is formed into a beak and used for sucking fluids. In some species the females have ovipositors with which they lay eggs in plants, whereas other species are parthenogenetic. In all cases the insects can multiply rapidly. They are classed as Exopterygota because there is only a partial metamorphosis during the development.

Thrips feed by scraping away the surface of the food source to gain access to the fluid which is exposed. This is generally the sap of plants, although certain species feed off fungi and some feed off insects. Because thrips are small and often live in the centre of flowers they are seldom noticed, but most plants are visited by these insects.

During close, thundery weather thrips often fly, forming small clouds a few feet above the ground. It is during such periods that most people have experienced the misfortune of getting a 'fly in the eye'. One of the common names given to thrips is Thunder Fly.

Although the insect serves a useful purpose in helping to pollinate plants, it is more often considered a pest due to the damage it causes. Apart from the collapse of plants cells caused by its method of feeding, thrips can also transfer various virus diseases. The existence of *Thrips tabaci* (not included in this book) in Saudi Arabia makes it virtually impossible to grow onions without the use of pesticides.

Aeolothripidae (Banded Thrips)

FEBRUARY – APRIL

***Aeolothrips deserticola* Priesner** (Desert Thrips)
There are a number of different species to be found in Arabia, but since most of them are very small and similar in appearance this book will not attempt classification. This species is one of the larger and more colourful thrips found. Prefers plant leaves to flower heads for its food source. Colonies sometimes reach pest proportions and ornamental plants such as *Ipomoea* (Morning Glory) are especially prone to attack.

×5

Neuroptera
(Lacewings and Antlions)

Both larvae and the adult insects are predators. Larvae are equipped with pincer-like mandibles that can grip the prey. Some species eat the victim, whereas other species suck the prey dry. The order Neuroptera contains a number of primitive families, but they all undergo a full metamorphosis during their life-cycle and are classified as endopterygote insects. Most of the species are nocturnal. The adult insects have compound eyes and also some have ocelli. The adults have 2 pairs of flimsy wings that are large and usually similar. Their complex wing venation is characteristic of the order and a guide to classification.

Ascalaphidae (Ascalaphids)

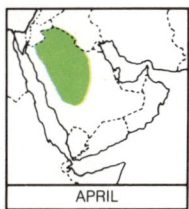
APRIL

***Bubopsis hamata* Klug** (Yellow Fleck) The habits of this family differ from the majority of other families contained in the Neuroptera. Adult Ascalaphids are strong fliers and hunt during the day. Larvae are predatory ground dwellers that actively hunt down prey. There are many different species of this family in Arabia, with *B. hamata* being the most widespread in the central area. They frequent desert steppe terrain, where the adult often sits on a branch of low vegetation waiting to catch other insects in flight. In this respect their activities are very similar to the Odonata (Dragonflies). The long, clubbed antennae of the Ascalaphids make them easy to distinguish from dragonflies, which have very small antennae.

♂

Nemopteridae (Ribbonwings)

APRIL – JUNE

***Halter halteratus* Forskål** (Knotted Halterwing) Sometimes at dusk in sandy areas swarms of small insects can be seen rising and falling in the air just above the ground. Most of these insects belong to the Neuropteridae and some are *H. halteratus*. The long filament on hindwings acts as a stabiliser during these almost stationary flights. Larvae feed on small insects in animal burrows and under stones.

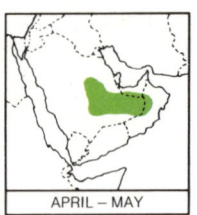
APRIL – MAY

***Dielocroce* spp.** (Threadwings) A number of species in the genus *Dielocroce* are found in Arabia, but their appearance and habits are very similar. The insects swarm in the same way as *Halter halteratus* (Knotted Halterwing), but their numbers are generally larger. *Dielocroce elegans* is the species most often encountered.

Chrysopidae (Lacewings)

MARCH – APRIL

***Chrysoperla carnea* Stephens** (Green Lacewing) This insect is often attracted to lights at night and may settle on the wall of a room where its attractive colours seldom fail to draw attention. The burnished gold of the eyes forms a striking contrast to the pale green of body and wings. Flight is weak and they spend most of the time among vegetation, where they prey on small insects. Females lay eggs on wax stalks to protect them from small predators. Larvae have sharp jaws and prey on aphids and other small insects. The species is widespread and has a distribution that extends to Europe and Britain. In Arabia it frequents gardens and oases and clumps of *Tephrosia*, where strong colonies of aphids often develop. Despite its weak flight, the adult is rarely attacked as it possesses a powerful defence mechanism. When roughly handled, the insect's body emits a foul-smelling liquid. There are several other members of the Chrysopidae family in Arabia, but *C. carnea* is the most common.

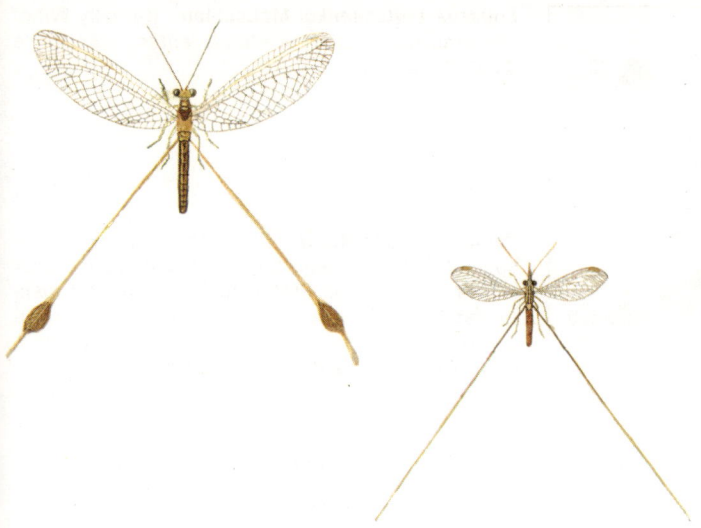

Myrmeleontidae (Antlions)

Most species of antlion are nocturnal. They could be mistaken for dragonflies, but may be distinguished by their antennae. Adult antlions have short sturdy antennae with clubs at the ends. Adults and larvae live on small insects. Larvae can be found in sandy habitats, where they dig a conical pit approximately 25 mm deep and 25 mm in diameter at ground level. They bury themselves at the bottom of the pit with only their jaws visible. Small insects, such as ants, fall into the pit and are unable to climb the loose sides. As the victim attempts to clamber out, it is bombarded with fine sand particles ejected by the antlion. Finally the victim tumbles to the bottom of the cone where it is seized by the sickle-shaped jaws of the larva, which then proceeds to suck the victim dry.

JULY – AUGUST

Gepus invisus **Navás** (Hunchback Antlion)   The adult has glossy hump in the centre of the thorax. It likes a sandy habitat.

APRIL – SEPTEMBER

***Lopezus fedtschenkoi* McLachlan** (Streaky Wing)
The wing markings of the adult *L. fedtschenkoi* make it easy to identify.

JULY – SEPTEMBER

***Palpares dispar* Navás** (Polkadot Antlion) Four species of this genus are found in Arabia, but *P. dispar* is the most common. Prefers rocky ravines and oasis fringes, where white seed-like eggs are laid in neat rows on flowers or grass stems. Larvae, when they hatch, drop to the ground and immediately proceed to dig a pit.

MAY

***Myrmecaelurus laetus* Klug** (Elegant Antlion)
Occurs in silty depressions in open rock desert.

SEPTEMBER – OCTOBER

***Ganguilus pallescens* Navás** (Longlegged Antlion)   The long legs permit easy identification.

SEPTEMBER

***Centroclisis cervina* Gerstäcker** (Hairy Antlion)
Commonly found in oasis fringes and desert farms where it often flies by day if disturbed. In cold weather it vibrates its wings to 'warm up' before flying.

APRIL – MAY

Nophis teillardi Navás (The Serpent) A number of species of this genus are found throughout the area. All are similar to *N. teillardi* and have the peculiar kink in the abdomen. Flight patterns are weak, so they seldom fly during windy weather.

Larva and pits

Lepidoptera
(Moths and Butterflies)

The word Lepidoptera is derived from two Greek words meaning scales and wings. This is a very apt description because the order is distinguished from all other orders by the wing membranes which are covered in minute scales. The scales are generally considered to be a special adaptation of the hairs found on less highly developed insects. Most scales are hollow and often contain pigments which provide colour. Although Lepidoptera appear to be very delicate, they have proved to be a remarkably successful order and there are approximately 120 000 known species in the world.

Most moths and butterflies possess a coiled proboscis which acts as a flexible trunk for the intake of liquid food, often nectar and water. During the immature or larval (caterpillar) stage of development most larvae feed on vegetation, but some species feed on aphids or ant larvae. Because of the enormous difference between the mature and the immature stages in the life of these insects, they are classified under the division of Endopterygota. They undergo a complete metamorphosis and the life-cycle comprises 4 different stages: ovum (egg), larva (caterpillar), pupa (chrysalis) and imago (moth or butterfly).

Sphingidae (Hawkmoths)

FEBRUARY–SEPTEMBER

Acherontia styx **Westwood** (Eastern Death's-Head Hawkmoth) A great deal of superstition surrounds the Death's-Head Hawkmoth, probably prompted by the dorsal markings on the thorax which resemble a skull and also the insect's ability to squeak if disturbed. Larvae can also make a noise. This appearance and behaviour are interpreted by the superstitious as an ill omen. *Acherontia styx* is common in most major towns and oases in coastal areas between Qatif in Saudi Arabia and Muscat in Oman. Larvae feed on plants of the nightshade family (potato, tomato, etc.) as well as on jasmines and *Clerodendron inerme*. Whole hedges of *Clerodendron* are often defoliated in Ras Tanura and Dhahran. Recently, this species has also colonised central and western Saudi Arabia where larvae can be found on *Tecoma, Duranta, Vitex, Lantana* and many other garden shrubs.

APRIL – OCTOBER

Acherontia atropos **Linnaeus** (Western Death's-Head Hawkmoth) Far less common than *A. styx* (Eastern Death's-Head Hawkmoth); the ranges of the two species do not normally overlap. Can be identified by presence of white central spot to the forewings and broad black bands across the underside of the abdomen. Foodplant of larvae similar to that of *A. styx*. (Not illustrated.)

×0.75

pupa

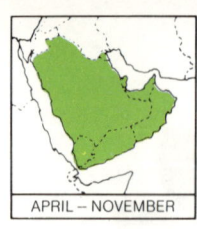

APRIL – NOVEMBER

***Agrius convolvuli* Linnaeus** (Convolvulus Hawkmoth) Wingspan is one of the largest for an insect in Arabia and may attain 150 mm (6 in.). A powerful migrant, often congregating in large numbers at dusk. Most adult moths obtain food by sucking nectar from flowers using a hollow proboscis, which projects from the head and is normally coiled up like a watch-spring when not in use. Length of proboscis varies according to species of moth. In the case of *A. convolvuli* it can extend to approximately 100 mm (4 in.), which permits the moth to extract nectar from long, trumpet-shaped flowers. It does not land to feed, but hovers in front of the flower while the proboscis penetrates to the nectar source. During the pupal stage of development, its proboscis is housed in an extension below the head. Larvae feed on *Ipomoea pes-caprae* (Morning Glory) and *Convolvulus* spp., especially those plants found in ornamental gardens. The large caterpillar looks quite ferocious, with a tail-horn resembling a sting, which is a harmless decoy meant to deceive would-be predators.

pupa

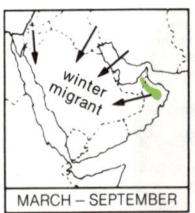

MARCH – SEPTEMBER

***Macroglossum stellatarum* Linnaeus** (Hummingbird Hawkmoth) Not resident in Saudi Arabia, but migrates from Northern Oman and Iran where it breeds. Larvae feed on *Galium* and *Gaillonia*. The adult flies during the day and bears a striking resemblance to a small hummingbird as it hovers while feeding in front of flowers.

green form

City Park, Al-Kharj, Saudi Arabia

JANUARY – JULY

***Daphnis nerii* Linnaeus** (Oleander Hawkmoth) Its colours act as perfect camouflage during the day when it rests among foliage. Visits gardens at night in search of flowers with nectar and to lay eggs on Oleander bushes. Larvae can be so common that they will defoliate a bush. When the larva is disturbed it will usually puff up the front body segments which greatly enlarge a pair of eyespots. These large false eyes are often sufficient to frighten away a potential predator. **A**

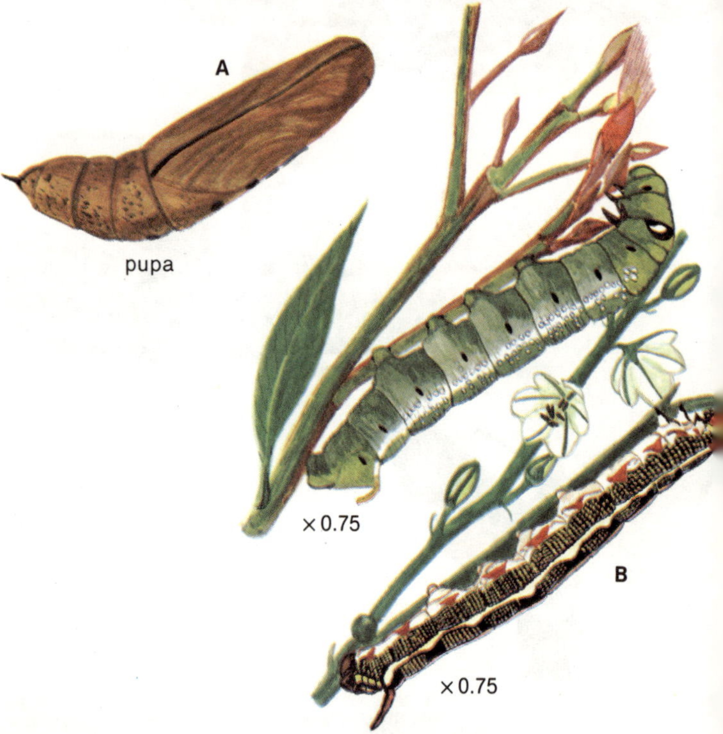

A

pupa

× 0.75

B

× 0.75

DECEMBER – MAY

***Hyles livornica* Esper** (Striped Hawkmoth) The most common Hawkmoth in Arabia, it is an insect of the open desert where it breeds on a variety of plants, but prefers *Asphodelus*, *Rumex* and *Calligonum*. Flies at night and migrates to other countries, some reaching as far north as Scandinavia. A successful breeding season with vast numbers of moths may occur after a period of heavy rain when numerous individuals can be seen visiting *Lycium* flowers in the late afternoon. **B**

Hippotion celerio Linnaeus (Silver-striped Hawkmoth) A migrant generally confined to oases, where the larvae feed on grapevine leaves and *Rumex*.

Nerium oleander

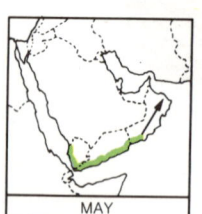

Cephonodes hylas Linnaeus (Coffee Clearwing) A day-flying Hawkmoth which is a migrant to northern Oman from Dhofar (southern Oman). When sucking nectar from flowers it expands and contracts the anal brush of hair as an aid to balance while it hovers. These hairs act in a similar manner to the tail feathers of a hovering bird such as a Kestrel.

Noctuidae (Owlet Moths)

The Noctuidae is the largest family in the order Lepidoptera. Most of the moths are brown or grey, although some have white, yellow or red hindwings. Mainly nocturnal, most species have tympanic organs on the thorax, which permit them to hear an approaching bat or bird. When this happens many fly erratically or fall to the ground. The larvae feed on low vegetation; some on grass and others are pests to agriculture. Most larvae are smooth with few hairs.

***Agrotis sardzeana* Brandt** (Autumn Sword Grass)
Favours dried grassland in sandy desert areas.

***Agrotis ipsilon* Hufnagel** (Dark Sword Grass) Common throughout the area and its range extends through Europe to Britain. The larvae commonly known as cutworms and feed on a number of plants and can be a pest to agriculture.

***Euxoa canariensis* Rebel** (Canary Island Dart) A number of similar species of the genus *Euxoa* occur in Arabia, but *E. canariensis* is the most common. Larvae generally feed on grass and can be a pest on lawns.

OCTOBER – APRIL

***Discestra sociabilis* Graslin** (White Spotted Nutmeg)   Several very similar species of the genus *Discestra* exist in Arabia, but *D. sociabilis* is found in both agricultural and urban areas.

APRIL – MAY

***Mythimna loreyi* Duponchel** (Single-line Wainscot) Numerous similar species of the genus *Mythimna* exist in Arabia, although *M. loreyi* is the most widespread and common.

FEBRUARY – APRIL

***Metopoceras omar* Oberthür** (Snow Leopard)   A species of the *Rhanterium* steppes which stretch from central Saudi Arabia across Kuwait and into Iraq.

FEBRUARY – APRIL

***Metopoceras delicata* Staudinger** (Pink Panther) Similar habits to *M. omar* (Snow Leopard) and both species may be found flying together. The shade of pink varies for *M. delicata* according to locality.

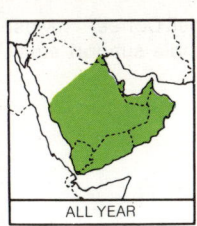

***Spodoptera littoralis* Boisduval** (Cotton Leafworm)
A serious pest of the cotton crop in Egypt. In Arabia, although common in agricultural areas, it rarely causes a problem. Larvae feed on a number of plants including lucerne and spinach.

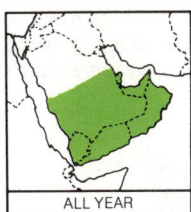

***Spodoptera exigua* Hübner** (Lesser Leafworm) Found in agricultural areas.

***Spodoptera cilium* Guenée** (Brown Spotted Lesser Leafworm) Flies with *S. exigua* (Lesser Leafworm). Can be identified by the grey brown spot on forewing, whereas *S. exigua* has an orange spot.

***Hadjina viscosa* Freyer** (Shimmerwings) Fringes of oases are the favourite habitat. Larvae feed on *Pluchea*. Adult always has the appearance that it has lost most of its wing scales.

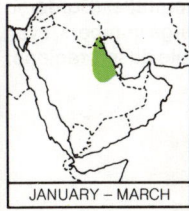

***Rhabinopteryx subtilis* Mabille** (Striped Grey) This is a suburban species that prefers gardens.

***Dysmilichia bicolor* Chrétien** (Irish Coffee)   Most rocky wadis in central Saudi Arabia support small populations of this moth.

***Heliothis nubigera* Herrich-Schäffer** (Nubian Straw) At certain times of the year, members of this genus are among the most common moths found in Arabia. After rain in the desert has encouraged a mass emergence, swarms of *H.nubigera* can be seen in gardens probing flowers for nectar or flying around street lights in towns. The black-spotted larvae feed on most low-growing herbs, but show a preference for *Zygophyllum simplex* (Dwarf Caltrops).

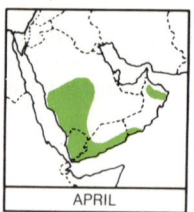

***Heliothis armigera* Hübner** (Dark Clover)   Found in rocky ravines of hilly areas, this is one of the rarer members of the genus.

***Heliothis peltigera* Denis & Schiffermüller** (Bordered Straw)   Common and found in large numbers, even in the most remote and inhospitable desert regions.

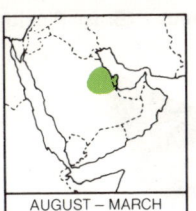
AUGUST – MARCH

***Rhodocleptria incarnata* Freyer** (Mouldy Straw) A rare species that favours *Rhanterium* steppe.

MARCH – MAY

***Masalia albida* Hampson** (False Wainscot) Always appears to have lost half its scales. There are a number of species in this genus that can be found in Arabia and all look very similar.

MARCH – APRIL

***Acontia biskrensis* Oberthür** (Variable Four Spot) Extremely variable in coloration, some being dark brown, others almost pure white. It is usually found in the company of *Metopoceras omar* (Snow Leopard) and *M. delicata* (Pink Panther) on fringes of oases.

JANUARY – MAY

***Acontia lucida* Hufnagel** (Lucid Four Spot) It is uncommon but has a widespread distribution.

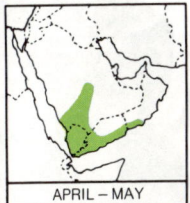
APRIL – MAY

***Chrysodeixis chalcites* Esper** (Giant Gem) There was confusion regarding the identity of this moth until recently. It was established by E. P. Wiltshire in 1982 as the only *Chrysodeixis* species found to date in Saudi Arabia.

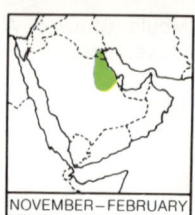

Cornutiplusia circumflexa Linnaeus (Brass Plusia) Uncommon.

Trichoplusia ni Hübner (Ni Moth) Common and found in oases throughout area. Generally found with another very common species of the genus, *T. daubei* Boisd (not included in this book), which is similar in appearance. Migrates across Europe and has been found in Britain. Larvae of both species feed on numerous plants.

Earias vittella Fabricius (Okra Pea Moth) A number of species of the genus *Earias* occur in Arabia and some are serious pests to agriculture. Larvae of *E. vittella* feed in Okra pods making them unfit for human consumption. Adults are sexually dimorphic and differ in shape and colour. A male is illustrated.

Dysgonia torrida Guenée (Coffee and Cream Moth) An oases species that frequents low vegetation where it feeds from flowers and fallen fruit.

OCTOBER – JANUARY

***Remigia frugalis* Fabricius** (Oasis Streak) Very common among grass in oases, where it flies during the day. Often rests on the ground and, when disturbed, readily takes flight.

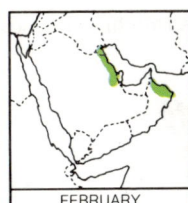
FEBRUARY

***Ophiusa tirhaca* Cramer** (Yellow Hindwing) Colour varies in intensity according to dryness of habitat. Generally found in gardens. Range extends into Europe, but the moth is uncommon there.

APRIL – MAY

***Clytie benenotata* Warren** (Shady Shades) Usual habitat is salt flats and oases fringes. Larvae feed on *Tamarix*.

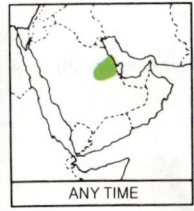
ANY TIME

***Clytie sancta* Staudinger** (Ochre Hindwing) Scarce and restricted to sandy areas in proximity to salt flats.

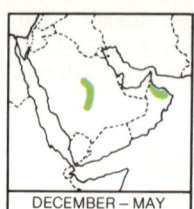

***Heteropalpia exarata* Mabille** (Dark Snout) Frequents valleys and wadis where it flies at night.

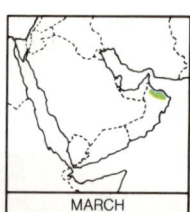

***Pericyma signata* Brandt** (Marbled Moth) Found in rocky ravines and depressions.

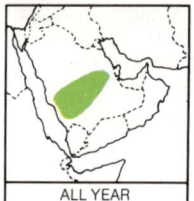

***Tytroca fasciolata* Warren** (Layered Moth) Common and widespread.

***Gnamptonyx innexa* Walker** (Brown White Spot) Inhabits scrub desert. Larvae feed on *Acacia* leaves.

***Drasteria habibazel* Dumont** (Marblecake Moth) A species of large, rocky wadis.

APRIL – OCTOBER

***Rhynchodontodes revolutalis* Zeller** (Lined Snout)   Several similar species of the genus *Rhynchodontodes* occur in Arabia. *Rhynchodontodes revolutalis* is common and attracted in large numbers to lights on walls surrounding villas.

MARCH – SEPTEMBER

***Anumeta asiatica* Wiltshire** (Asiatic Sand Moth) Inhabits sand dunes where clumps of grass and *Cyperus conglomeratus* (Desert Papyrus) grow.

NOVEMBER – MARCH

***Anumeta hilgerti* Rothschield**   *(Dark Sand Moth)* Inhabits sand dune areas.

SEPTEMBER – APRIL

***Acrobyla kneuckeri* Rebel**   (Shadow Moth)   Prefers silty desert depressions and scrub desert.

***Drasteriodes limata* Christoph** (Creamcake) Usual habitat is rocky ravines.

JANUARY – MARCH

***Armada panaceorum* Ménétriès** (Rock Moth)
Rock-strewn plains form its usual habitat. It is well camouflaged when it settles on rocks where it spends the day, but readily takes flight if disturbed.

***Emmelia trabealis* Scopoli** (Spotted Sulphur) A species of central Europe, it is at the extremity of its range in Arabia. Frequents oases where the larvae feed on *Convolvulus arvensis*.

***Autophila cymaenotaenia* Boursin** (Burnt Speck)
This and a similar species, *A. cerealis,* frequent rock-strewn desert. When disturbed they do not generally take to flight, but prefer to run to the nearest cover.

***Thria robusta* Walker** (Thickneck) Inhabits dense scrub desert.

***Cerocala sana* Staudinger** (Labyrinth Moth) This moth looks like a Geometrid. Larvae feed on *Helianthemum*.

Arctiidae (Tiger Moths)

Many of the species in the family Arctiidae are brightly coloured which is often an indication that they are poisonous. Most diurnal predators will not attack insects with warning coloration. Some of the moths are also capable of emitting high-frequency sounds which are used to jam the 'radar' of attacking bats. The larvae usually have hairs which can cause severe irritation to unprotected skin. These hairs are often also incorporated in the silken cocoon to protect the pupa.

***Utetheisa pulchella* Linnaeus** (Crimson Speckled Footman) Conspicuous and common day-flying moth throughout Arabia, often very abundant in both deserts and oases wherever species of *Heliotropium*, the larval foodplants, are common.

***Spilosoma arabica* Hampson** (Arabian Ermine) Frequents rocky wadis that contain *Astragalus spinosus* (Spiny Milk Vetch), the larval foodplant.

Lymantriidae (Tussock Moths)

ALL YEAR

***Casama innotata* Walker** (Acacia Tussock Moth) Rock-strewn desert with groups of *Acacia* trees provide the habitat for this species which is often found in the company of *Spilosoma arabica* (Arabian Ermine). Larvae feed on *Acacia*.

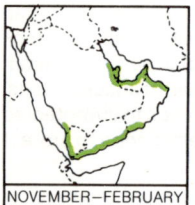

NOVEMBER–FEBRUARY

***Euproctis cervina* Walker** (Canary Vapourer) The male starts to fly in the middle of the afternoon in search of a female that is prepared to mate. This search may continue through most of the night. The female lays eggs on *Terminalia catappa* (Indian Almond), a common garden tree, although the species is also known to feed on *Alhagi*.

 ♂

Lasiocampidae (Eggars)

Most larvae in the family Lasiocampidae are covered in hairs. These hairs often contain a mild poison and it is advisable to handle them with gloves as they can cause severe irritation. The larvae pupate underground in silk cocoons.

OCTOBER

***Chondrostega fasciata* Staudinger** (Red Streak) The male closely resembles a large white *Euproctis cervina* (Canary Vapourer) and during late afternoon may be seen quartering the ground for wingless females. Favourite foodplants are *Trigonella* and *Rhanterium*. After spring rains, when the deserts are green, large numbers of the bright red-banded larvae can be found in certain localities.

 ♀

cocoon

FEBRUARY – MAY

***Chilena laristana* Daniel** (Tippler Moth) Common but rarely seen, as it frequents remote sand dune areas. Larval foodplant is *Calligonum comosum* (Desert Knotgrass). During April, larvae are conspicuous on the leafless plants. The species has been given the common name 'Tippler' due to the habit of the larvae which drink beads of dew on the plant.

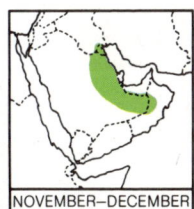

NOVEMBER–DECEMBER

***Autosphyla henkei* Staudinger** (Desert Knotgrass Eggar) A rare moth of the sand dunes. Larvae feed on *Calligonum comosum* (Desert Knotgrass). They are gregarious and occur in large numbers which often strip the foodplant; they also spin silk webs for protection.

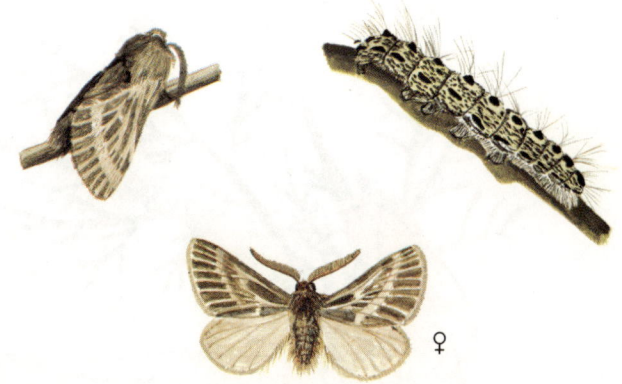

SEPTEMBER

***Lasiocampa serrula* Guenée** (Grey Eggar)   Prefers sand dunes and rock outcrops which have richer vegetation.

MARCH – OCTOBER

***Streblote siva* Lefèbvre** (Jujube Lappet)   The most common member of the Lasiocampidae family found in Arabia. Larvae feed on a variety of foodplants that include *Zizyphus*, *Tamarix*, *Avicennia marina* and *Punica*. Larvae can be so numerous that they defoliate complete branches of trees, leaving only papery cocoons on bare twigs.

68

Geometridae (Looper Moths)

Insects comprising the family Geometridae appear frail, but are successful and prolific. Adults have tympanals which enable them to detect the presence of bats. The larvae (or inch-worms) have 2 pairs of prolegs near the rear of their abdomen. These are used to clasp a twig before the larva stretches out to find a hold for the legs on its thorax. Having obtained a grip, the rear pair of legs are drawn up to a position immediately behind the forelegs. To do this the body has to form a loop, which gives the insect its common name, 'looper', and describes its method of locomotion. The larvae often resemble a twig of the foodplant.

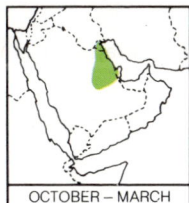

OCTOBER – MARCH

***Pingasa lahayei* Oberthür** (Willow Beauty) Although *P. lahayei* is the most common, there are many similar species of the genus *Pingasa* found in Arabia. Frequents oases and gardens where larvae generally feed on *Salix* spp. and other shrubs.

MAY

***Hyperythra muselmana* Brandt** (Burnt Thorn) Inhabits desert farms fringed with *Tamarix*.

NOVEMBER – MAY

***Chlorissa discessa* Walker** (Jasmine Emerald) Its distinctive colour provides good camouflage when the moth rests on vegetation. Larvae feed on hedging plant *Clerodendron inerme*.

NOVEMBER – MAY

Tephrina disputaria Guenée (Acacia Looper) One of the most common moths in Arabia. Larvae feed on *Acacia*. At rest the moth folds its wings above the body similar to butterflies. Male differs from female in the number of brown-coloured streaks on the forewings.

♀

OCTOBER – MARCH

Gnophos subvariegatus Staudinger (Desert Annulet) A common cold-weather moth.

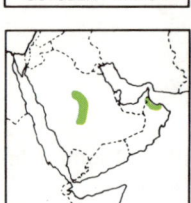

MARCH

Epirrhoe wiltshirei Brandt (Wiltshire's Carpet) A rare species confined to well-vegetated desert wadis.

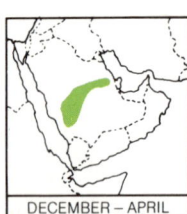

DECEMBER – APRIL

Zamarada hyalinaria Guenée (Rubbed Wing) Has the appearance that it has lost many of its wing scales.

NOVEMBER – MAY

Hemidromodes sabulifera Prout (Pink Carpet) A common moth usually overlooked due to its small size.

Lithostege notata Bang-Haas (Striped Swiftwing) Has a very unusual shape to wings. Frequents rock-strewn wadis.

Lithostege palaestinensis Amsel (Grey Swiftwing) A northern species which only flies during the colder winter months.

Eupithecia ultimaria Boisduval (Scalloped Pug) The resting position of this moth is typical of all Pugs. Wings are extended at right angles to the body and pressed flat against the background on which it is resting.

Rhodometra sacraria Linnaeus (Vestal) Common in oases and towns, it migrates and has been recorded in Britain.

Lantana camara

71

Cossidae (Goat and Leopard Moths)

The family Cossidae contains a number of large and primitive moths. Larvae bore into the wood of living trees or into stems of plants, thus obtaining protection from most predators.

APRIL – JUNE

***Holcocerus gloriosus* Erschov** (Ermine Leopard) Favourite habitat for this moth is grass-covered sand dunes and hollows.

NOVEMBER – AUGUST

***Lamellocossus aries* Püngeler** (Arabian Goatmoth) Rare and frequents oasis fringes. Coloration varies according to locality.

Pterophoridae (Plume Moths)

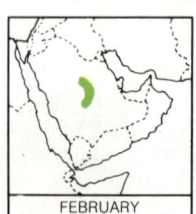

FEBRUARY

***Emmelina monodactyla* Linnaeus** (Grey Feather Moth) Wings of moths in this family are divided up into 3 or 4 plumes similar to feathers. *Emmelina monodactyla* is the most common of several similar species found in Arabia.

Pyralidae (Pyralid Moths)

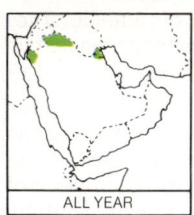

ALL YEAR

***Ephestia kuehniella* Zeller** (Mediterranean Flour Moth) One of the most serious pests in Arabia, as the larvae feed on stored grain, flour and dried fruit in granaries, flour mills and stores. Food not eaten by the larvae is made unfit for human consumption by silk webs of the larvae.

FEBRUARY – MAY

***Nomophila noctuella* Denis & Schiffermüller** (Rush Veneer) Common and prefers oases and desert steppe. Larvae can be very numerous feeding on grass and lucerne which they cover with silk webs.

MARCH – MAY

***Lamoria anella* Denis & Schiffermüller** (Grey Slipper) One of several similar species of the genus *Lamoria* found in Arabia. It frequents oases fringes and well-vegetated depressions on stone-strewn plains.

OCTOBER – MAY

***Cornifrons ulceratalis* Lederer** (Common Ulcer) Common, it prefers open desert and oases fringes.

Hesperiidae (Skipper Butterflies)

The family Hesperiidae is considered to be a distinct group of butterflies. They appear to form a link between moths and butterflies, as they have certain characteristics common to both.

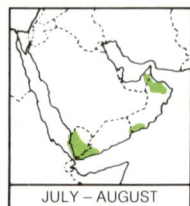
JULY – AUGUST

***Coeliades anchises* Gerstäcker** (Giant Skipper) Common on the wadi floors of northern Oman, but has not yet been discovered in eastern Saudi Arabia. Larvae (caterpillars) occupy silk-lined, rolled-up leaves of the foodplant *Acridocarpus*, which protects them from ants.

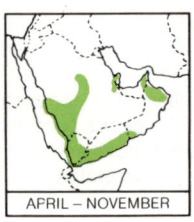
APRIL – NOVEMBER

***Spialia doris* Walker** (Aden Skipper) Frequents wadi floors and desert depressions with plenty of vegetation. The markings of the butterfly act as good camouflage which combined with its fast flight make it extremely difficult to detect. A flash of grey and silver as the wings catch the light is often all that is seen. Feeds on *Convolvulus histrix* (Spiny Bindweed).

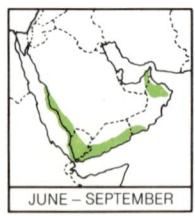
JUNE – SEPTEMBER

***Gomalia elma* Trimen** (African Mallow Skipper) Although common in south-west Saudi Arabia, to date it has only been found in northern Oman and the United Arab Emirate of eastern Arabia. Inhabits oases and fertile wadis. In contrast to other skippers, holds all 4 wings at 45° when sunning itself. Most skippers when at rest lay the hindwings flat but keep the forewings close together in a vertical position. Foodplant is *Arbutilon*.

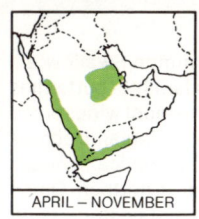
APRIL – NOVEMBER

Gegenes nostrodamus Fabricius (Peaty Skipper) Common in oases and farms across eastern Arabia. Hard to detect due to rapid flight and good camouflage. Larva feeds on grasses. Occasionally adults found feeding in considerable numbers on flowers of *Lantana*.

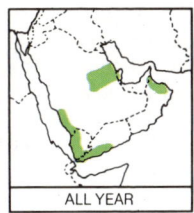
ALL YEAR

Pelopidas thrax Hübner (Millet Skipper) Where this species is found it occurs in good numbers. Has the short, fast flight characteristic of most species in this family and the reason for the common name of 'Skipper'. Foodplant is grasses, but the butterfly particularly enjoys feeding from flowers of *Lantana*.

♂

APRIL – NOVEMBER

Pelopidas mathias Fabricius (Lesser Millet Skipper) Prefers dry wadis, although large numbers are attracted to the flowers of alfalfa when this is grown on nearby farms. Range does not normally overlap that of *Pelopidas thrax* (Millet Skipper). Male is identified by androconial scent scales which appear as a streak on the forewings and are not present in female. The larvae feed on grasses.

Wadi Hanifah, Riyadh, Saudi Arabia

Papilionidae (Swallowtail Butterflies)

OCTOBER – APRIL

Papilio machaon Linnaeus (Common Swallowtail) Swallowtails are the oldest known family of butterflies in the world. *Papilio machaon* is the most widespread species in the family, and occurs in England, across Europe, North Africa, Asia and North America. In Arabia there are two subspecies: *muetingi*, in northern Oman and *syriacus,* in the Al Hasa Oasis of eastern Saudi Arabia. The latter subspecies is illustrated. The Butterfly is attracted to many flowers, but is especially fond of sipping nectar from *Ocimum basilicum* (Sweet Basil). Caterpillars feed exclusively on plants in the carrot and orange families such as *Foeniculum, Ruta, Ammi majus* (False Bishops Weed) and *Haplophyllum*. They extract distasteful substances from the plants and when threatened emit these as a deterrent. The unpleasant fluid is secreted through a special retractable forked organ situated behind the head. (A related species, *P. saharae* Oberthür, occurs in western Arabia and may also inhabit the Jebel Tuwayq.)

FEBRUARY – NOVEMBER

Papilio demoleus Linnaeus (Citrus Swallowtail) During evolution this Swallowtail lost its tails but still maintains a graceful flight. Originally a native of Pakistan, it has spread from oasis to oasis as man has cultivated citrus fruits in eastern Arabia. Also it inhabits most major towns. Caterpillar feeds exclusively on the foliage of orange, lemon and lime trees and can be a pest when found in large numbers, especially in young plantations. *Papilio demodocus* Esper replaces *P. demoleus* in western Arabia.

× 1·25

pupa

× 1·25

× 1·25

Foeniculum vulgare (Fennel)

Pieridae (Whites and Sulphur Butterflies)

OCTOBER – MAY

***Artogeia rapae* Linnaeus** (Small White) The 'Cabbage White' butterfly of Europe, Asia and North America. In eastern and central Saudi Arabia, it is only an autumn migrant, but occasionally colonies are established in cabbage and radish fields where larvae (caterpillars) can become a pest. Colonies found in the Tuwayq Hills (subspecies *leucosoma*) are derived from Levantine stock. Colonies in Qatif and Tarut Island originated from Iranian stock (subspecies *iranica*); the latter is illustrated.

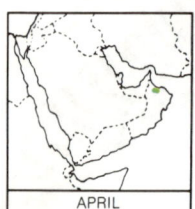

APRIL

***Artogeia krueperi* Staudinger** (Krueper's Small White) Distinguished from *A. rapae* (Small White) by much larger and darker wing markings. Has only been found at one locality in northern Oman (2100 m) although it is widely distributed from southern Europe to Pakistan. Larva feed on *Alyssum*.

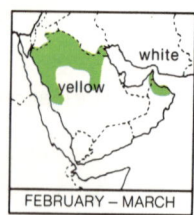

FEBRUARY – MARCH

***Elphinstonia charlonia* Donzel** (Greenish Black-Tip) Scarce and very local; frequents dry hillsides. Butterflies from different areas vary in ground colour, being either a greenish yellow or pure white. Those found in northern Oman are white and may be a separate species. Due to this variation in colour, the butterfly can look very similar to *Euchloe falloui* (Scarce Green Striped White). However, the hindwing underside of all forms of *E. charlonia* is almost completely green, in distinct contrast to *Euchloe falloui*. It has 2 broods. Foodplant of larvae is unknown, but possibly *Matthiola* or *Diplotaxis*.

JANUARY – MARCH

***Euchloe belemia* Esper** (Green Striped White) A true inhabitant of desert scrub and steppe of north-eastern Saudi Arabia. Greatly influenced by weather. In a wet year there may be 3 broods, whereas in a dry year there will be only 1. The small colony in the Qatif Oasis feeds on the seedpods of radish, which is unusual as the main foodplants are *Sinapis* and *Brassica*. **A**

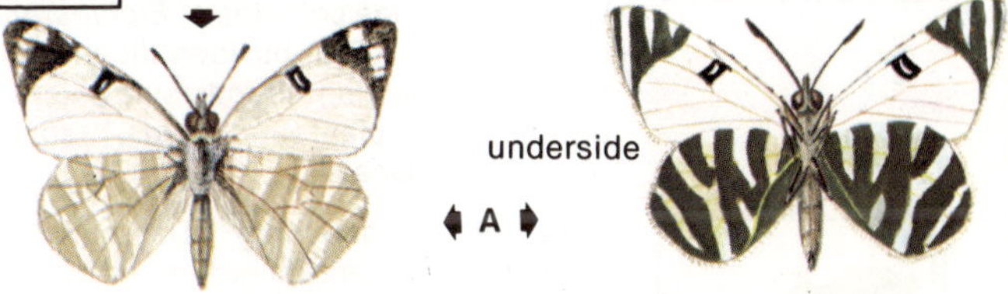

underside

◀ A ▶

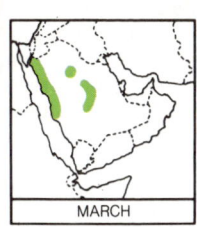

MARCH

***Euchloe falloui* Allard** (Scarce Green Striped White) A desert species which inhabits the sides of hot rocky wadis where the foodplant *(Moricandia sinaica)* grows. Although similar to *E.belemia* (Green Striped White) the two butterflies can be distinguished by the black discal spot on underside of the forewing. *Euchloe belemia* has a white centre to this spot, whereas *E.falloui* has a solid black spot. Not known to have more than 1 brood per year. **B**

MARCH

***Euchloe aegyptiaca* Verity** (Woad White) From above this butterfly looks very similar to its close relatives — *E. belemia* and *E. falloui*, however, the hindwing undersides are mottled rather than striped. It is a rare insect found only in the Jebel Shammar around Hail, where the larvae feed on *Isatis lusitanica* (Desert Woad).

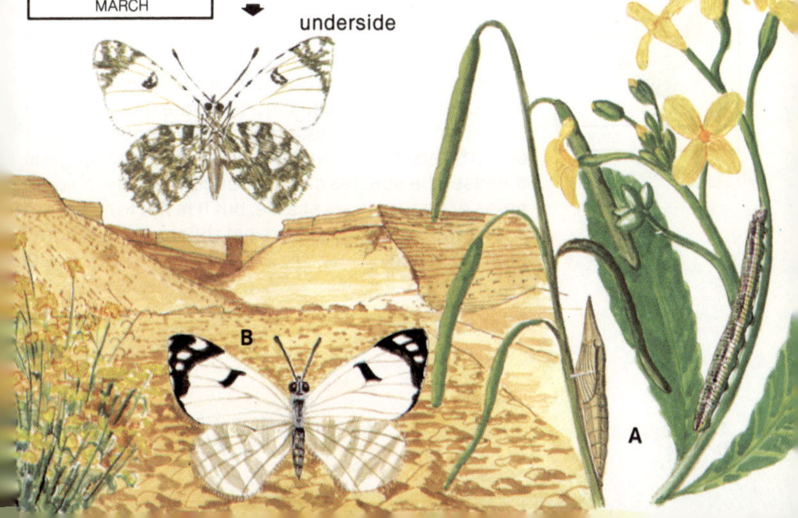

underside

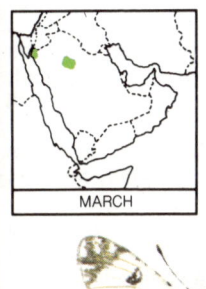

MARCH – DECEMBER

***Pontia daplidice* Linnaeus** (Bath White) Only truly resident in the high mountains of northern Oman, but a very strong flier and migrant. Common name refers to City of Bath in England where migratory specimens were captured during the eighteenth century. The upperside of the butterfly is very similar to *Pontia glauconome* (Desert White), *Euchloe belemia* (Green Striped White), *E. falloui* (Scarce Green Striped White) and some colonies of *Elphinstonia charlonia* (Greenish Black-Tip), but identification may be ascertained by inspecting the underside which is completely different. Foodplants are *Reseda, Arabis, Sinapis* and other Brassicaceae. **A**

MARCH – DECEMBER

***Pontia glauconome* Klug** (Desert White) Inhabitant of the desert and found throughout the Middle East and North Africa where it frequents sandhills, wadis, scrubland and mountainsides, but not normally oases. The upperside of the butterfly is very similar to *Euchloe belemia* (Green Striped White), *E. falloui* (Scarce Green Striped White) and some colonies of *Elphinstonia charlonia* (Greenish Black-Tip), but identification can easily be ascertained by inspecting the underside. Although it flies during the hotter months, its appearance is irregular, which may be due to choice of available food. Foodplants are *Ochradenus, Reseda, Dipterygium, Zilla, Moricandia,* etc. The black-spotted grey and white capterpillars feed on any of those plants and possibly several other plants, which gives the species a good chance of survival in a difficult environment. **B**

OCTOBER – MAY

***Anaphaeis aurota* Fabricius** (Brown-veined White) Common throughout Arabia and generally found in most oases and wadis. Migrates in spectacular numbers and butterflies lay eggs on *Capparis* and *Maerua* bushes. The vast number of larvae have been known to strip these plants in an oasis. When this happens some larvae (caterpillars) are unable to find sufficient food and, as a result, dwarf specimens of butterfly are not uncommon. Due to a bacteriological disease, the species can die out completely in some areas or become very scarce, but it is not long before a new influx of migrants re-establishes the colony. Multi-brooded. **C**

B   **A**   *Capparis spinosa* (Common Caper)

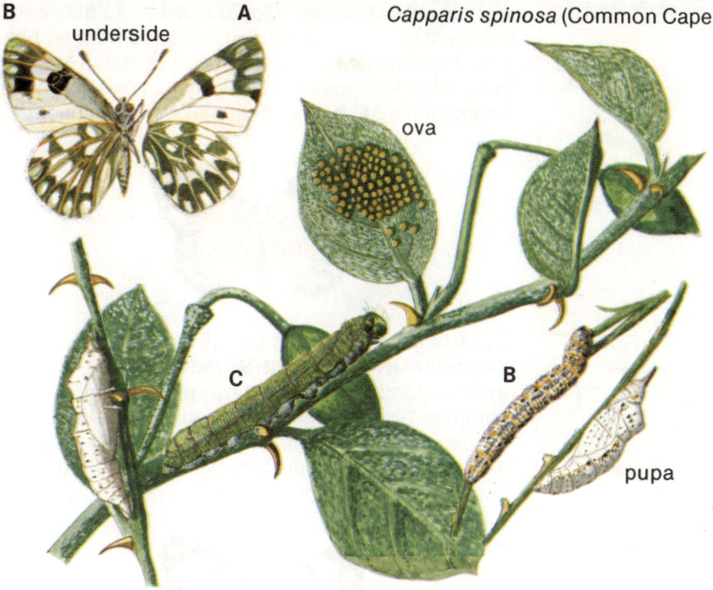

underside

ova

C

B

pupa

♂

C

underside

The Kuwait Towers, Kuwait City

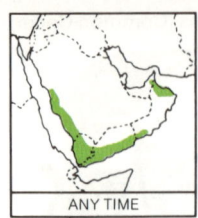

ANY TIME

***Colotis calais* Cramer** (Topaz Arab) To date only recorded from the coastal plain of northern Oman, but possibly exists in some parts of eastern Saudi Arabia. In suitable localities the butterfly can be abundant. Foodplant is *Salvadora persica* (Toothbrush bush).

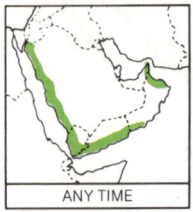

ANY TIME

***Colotis phisadia* Godart** (Blue-spotted Arab) Where the larval foodplant *(Salvadora persica)* occurs, this lively and attractive butterfly may be seen in large numbers. Ground colour of the female is variable, with specimens ranging from white to yellow and light pink. All female colour forms may be distinguished from males by heavier dark markings.

♂

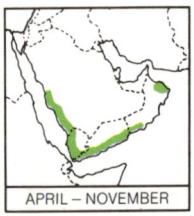

APRIL – NOVEMBER

***Colotis halimede* Klug** (Orange Patch White) Although widespread in south-western Arabia, to date there is only one known locality within the area covered by this book. It is found in the hot ravines of the Jebel Abu Da'ud in northern Oman where the foodplant, *Cadaba glandulosa* (Glandular Caperbush) of the larvae is available. The discovery of the foodplant in a new locality should provide a guide for further investigation. Only the male has yellow markings on the wings, female looks similar to male in all other respects.

♂

ANY TIME

***Colotis danae* Fabricius** (Scarlet Tip) Although common in western Saudi Arabia as far north as Yanbu, it has a very restricted distribution in eastern Arabia. It is confined to a small number of colonies around Basra (Iraq) and to a stretch of coastal plain in north Oman, between Seeb and Qurayat. The foodplant, *Cadaba farinosa* (Small-leaved Caperbush) is rare throughout the area and occurs in scattered localities. Consequently colonies of the insect may also be isolated from one another by several kilometres. Female is easily distinguished from male by heavier dark markings on forewings. The full-grown larva is 2 cm long and bluish green with a pale dorsal line. It is covered with hollow stubby bristles which produce a bitter orange fluid when agitated, an effective deterrent to predators, especially ants.

♂

MARCH – NOVEMBER

***Colotis liagore* Klug** (Sahel Orange Tip) It likes dry wadis and is attracted to flowers of *Acacia* around which it may often be found in large numbers. Limitation in range is due to the restricted location of *Maerua*, the main foodplant of the larvae, which also feed on *Capparis cartilagena* (Rock Caper). Female is similar to male, although generally has dark markings on the forewing. Occasionally heavy, black-banded specimens occur, as in specimen illustrated.

♀
dark form

♂

OCTOBER – MAY

***Colotis fausta* Olivier** (Salmon Arab) Distribution of this fast-flying butterfly is restricted by the discontinuous range of *Capparis*, the foodplant of the larva. The butterfly is a noted migrant and can be found on most *Capparis* plants. Female is more heavily marked than the male and both sexes vary in ground colour. Butterflies from oasis colonies tend to be salmon pink, whereas those from ravines and mountainous areas are generally light orange. **A**

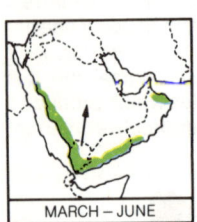
MARCH – JUNE

***Colotis chrysonome* Klug** (Golden Arab) Truly resident only along coastal plains of western Saudi Arabia and the Yemen. Occasionally, due to favourable conditions, large numbers of butterflies emerge and migrate east as far as Riyadh and northern Oman and may establish colonies on bushes of the foodplant, *Maerua crassifolia*. These colonies can survive for several years until there is a drought. The insects then disappear until another migration occurs.

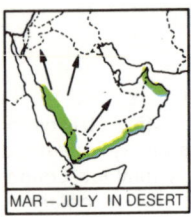
MAR – JULY IN DESERT

***Catopsilia florella* Fabricius** (African Migrant) Has a powerful flight and migrates over long distances. Resident in Egypt, North Africa, India and China. In eastern Arabia, it is truly resident only in gardens of northern Oman. Has continuous broods, and most years, mass migrations occur from western Saudi Arabia where the species is common. Some reach Riyadh and Al Kharj where they breed, the larvae feeding on the local *Cassia italica* (Dwarf Senna) shrubs. It is not yet established in central Saudi Arabia, the yearly migration accounts for its appearance in this area.

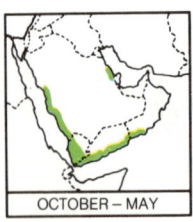
OCTOBER – MAY

***Eureme hecabe* Boisduval** (Common Grass Yellow) Has a range extending from Africa to Japan, but in eastern Arabia it is confined to Qatif Oasis and Tarut Island. Probably introduced into the Arabian Gulf with cargo conveyed by dhows from India. Foodplant of larvae is the yellow flowering *Sesbania aegyptiaca* (Pea Tree) which is also an introduced species. Larvae can be very numerous, although not easy to see due to excellent camouflage. The delicate pupa is normally hidden beneath a leaf in a silk girdle; the one illustrated is depicted just prior to hatching. Male and female butterfly look identical. **B**

Capparis spinosa (Common Caper)

Cassia italica (Dwarf Senna)

Sesbania aegyptiaca (Pea Tree)

OCTOBER – JUNE

***Colias croceus* Geoffroy** (Clouded Yellow) Before the cultivation of alfalfa (lucerne) as an animal fodder this butterfly was probably only a winter migrant to the Arabian Peninsula. Now established on most farms and oases throughout eastern and central Arabia. The larvae can be a pest as the insect multiplies rapidly to form very large populations. Foodplants are *Medicago, Sesbania* and *Trigonella*. When the butterflies are disturbed they fly up in large numbers giving the appearance of small puffs of yellow smoke. The colour of the butterfly varies considerably between sexes. The 2 main forms of male are orange and yellow. Female has 3 main forms, orange, white and yellow. All colour forms are illustrated, although normal form is orange. The frequency with which the other colour forms occur varies within different colonies. Within one known colony the white form occurred approximately once in 10 females and the yellow once in 50 females. The yellow form of male occurred approximately once in 50.

normal male

normal female

white form female

yellow form male

Lycaenidae (Blue Butterflies)

APRIL – NOVEMBER

***Apharitis acamas* Klug** (Leopard Butterfly) Very local and only flies for short periods. Lays eggs on plants frequented by *Cematogaster* ants, which visit the plants to obtain nectar. They are attracted to the larvae which they convey to their nest and rear as if they were ant larvae. The *A. acamas* larvae apparently feed on the ant larvae within the ants' nest. Two distinct subspecies occur in eastern Arabia. One is found in sandy hollows, while the other, a darker form, lives on edges of date plantations. The latter, which is illustrated, is subspecies *hypargyros*.

underside

APRIL – NOVEMBER

***Apharitis myrmecophila* Dumont** (Desert Leopard Butterfly) Haunts sand desert areas stabilized by colonies of the foodplant *Calligonum*. The butterfly varies in coloration and when in flight resembles a small fritillary. Few people have seen this species because of its short life-span and preference for walking or sitting rather than flying.

underside

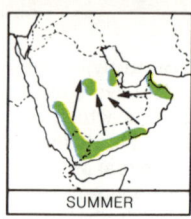
SUMMER

***Deudorix livia* Klug**   (Pomegranate Playboy)   Resident in western Arabia and mountains of northern Oman. Occasionally migrates and will colonise other areas until eliminated by unfavourable conditions. Foodplants are pomegranate, mimosa and dates, the larva feeding inside the fruit.

SUMMER

***Myrina silenus* Fabricius**   (Figtree Blue)   Although common in the Asir of western Saudi Arabia, to date it has only been found in northern Oman, but may exist in other parts of eastern Arabia. Foodplant is *Ficus salicifolia* (Willow-leaved Fig).

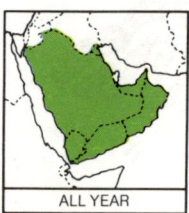
ALL YEAR

***Lampides boeticus* Linnaeus**   (Long-tailed Blue) Common and can be seen in short, fast flight over most fields of alfalfa. Also occurs in Southern Europe and has been recorded as a great rarity in Great Britain. Female lays china-white eggs singly at base of flowers. The tiny larva (caterpillar) usually bores directly into young seedpods of legumes, especially *Sesbania aegyptiaca* (Pea Tree), where it feeds until fully grown. The female butterfly is darker with fewer blue markings than the male. This difference in markings and colour between the sexes is a characteristic of the Lycaenidae family and often the butterflies appear unrelated.

MARCH — APRIL

***Pseudophilotes vicrama* Denis & Schiffermüller** (Baton Blue)   Although widely distributed in Eastern Europe and the Levant, *P. vicrama* is only found in the Musandam Peninsula of northern Oman. Here it frequents rocky slopes with low vegetation. Larval foodplant is unknown in Arabia, although European populations feed on *Thymus*.

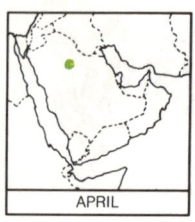
APRIL

***Pseudophilotes abencerragus* Pierret**   (False Baton Blue)   The Saudi Arabian population found in the Jebel Shammar around Hail, is a relict distribution from the last ice-age; the main population stretches from Jordan across the Sinai, Egypt and North Africa, to Spain. Confined to steep, rocky slopes strewn with *Isatis, Astragalus, Polygala* and scattered clumps of *Rhus tripartita*, where it flies very close to the ground.

underside

underside

underside

underside

The Tuwayq Hills, Al Hariq, Saudi Arabia

89

JANUARY – DECEMBER

***Tarucus rosaceus* Austaut** (Mediterranean Tiger Blue) Common in areas where *Zizyphus spina-christi* (Jujube tree) grows, in cultivated oases and settlements. Larvae feed on undersides of the leaves, forming transparent troughs through which light can be seen. The butterflies are often seen on *Heliotropium* plants, taking nectar. **A**

JANUARY – DECEMBER

***Tarucus balkanicus* Freyer** (Little Tiger Blue) Resembles *Tarucus rosaceus* (Mediterranean Tiger Blue) in size, shape and colour and has similar habits. However, larvae do not feed on leaves of the Jujube tree and are therefore not in competition with *T. rosaceus*. Since larvae feed only on *Zizyphus nummularia* (Desert Jujube) and *Z. lotus* (Small-leaved Jujube), the range of the butterfly is limited to the range of these shrubs, i.e. the Tuwayq Hills (April – November) and Qatar (all year).

APRIL – NOVEMBER

***Azanus ubaldus* Cramer** (Velvet Spotted Blue) Habitat is rocky deserts. Can generally be seen flying in and out of top branches of species of *Acacia* trees, especially *A. ehrenbergiana*, or taking nectar from the flowers. Has 2 broods, April – May and October – November. Common throughout its range.

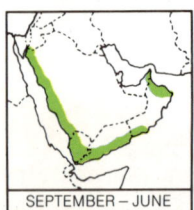
SEPTEMBER – JUNE

***Azanus jesous* Guérin-Méneville** (African Babul Blue) Found throughout North Africa, Egypt and Syria and looks similar to *A. ubaldus* (Velvet Spotted Blue). Where the ranges overlap, both species may be found flying together often around *Acacia* trees, the foodplant. Identification can be ascertained by inspecting underside markings of the wings. *Azanus ubaldus* has 2 black spots on costal margin of forewing. These spots are not present in *A. jesous*.

APRIL – NOVEMBER

***Anthene amarah* Guérin-Méneville** (Leaden Ciliate Blue) Local but widespread desert species often found in association with *Azanus ubaldus* (Velvet Spotted Blue) flying around *Acacia* trees, the foodplant. Male butterfly a much lighter shade of brown than female.

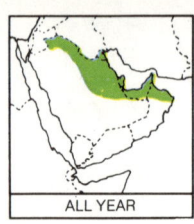
ALL YEAR

***Zizeeria karsandra* Moore** (Asian Grass Blue) Found throughout the whole area and generally abundant, which is remarkable since it has a very weak flight and is not a strong migrant. Considerable variation in the size of butterflies, probably due to the quantity and vigour of available foodplants, which are legumes, especially *Medicago sativa* (Alfalfa).

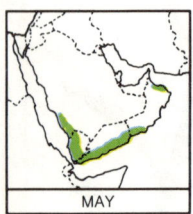
MAY

***Zizula hylax* Fabricius** (Gaica Blue) Looks similar to the last species, but prefers more fertile country. Although common in western Arabia, has only been found in northern Oman to date. Foodplant is *Oxalis*.

MARCH – APRIL

***Plebejus pylaon* Fischer** (Zephyr Blue) Rare and to date only found in the Tuwayq Hills and at Hail. Probably exists in isolated populations throughout northeastern Saudi Arabia. Nearest other known colonies are in Jordan. Generally occupies small hillside gullies containing foodplant, *Astragalus spinosus* (Spiny Milk Vetch).

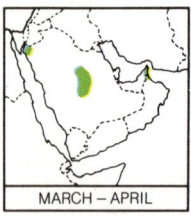
MARCH – APRIL

***Agrodiaetus loewii* Zeller** (Loew's Blue) Inhabits floors of dry wadis where the foodplant, *Astragalus spinosus* (Spiny Milk Vetch), grows. Often groups pass the night together on flower heads of *Teucrium oliverianum* (Desert Germander). Has rapid flight when disturbed, but generally returns to the same plants. Female butterfly has 2 colour forms, dark brown (illustrated) and blue which is similar to the male.

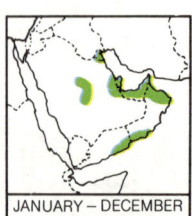
JANUARY – DECEMBER

***Chilades parrhasius* Fabricius** (Small Cupid) May be found flying in groups around the foodplant trees, *Acacia tortillis* (Tortuous Mimosa) and *Prosopis spicigera* (Mesquite) in the Tuwayq Hills (April – November) and Qatar (all year). Can be abundant, especially if good spring rains encourage prolific growth of the trees. Although fully grown larvae are green and yellow, as illustrated, young larvae are reddish brown with long backward pointing hairs and at this stage live in a cluster of closed leaves.

APRIL – NOVEMBER

***Chilades galba* Lederer** (Lederer's Cupid) Absence of 'tails' on the hindwings of male and female is the only way of distinguishing this species from *C. parrhasius* (Small Cupid). Larvae only feed on native *Prosopis spicigera* (Mesquite) and not on the introduced *Prosopis juli-flora* (Honey Mesquite), which probably accounts for its restricted range.

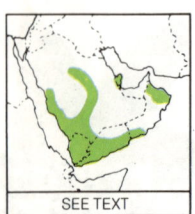

SEE TEXT

***Freyeria trochylus* Freyer** (Grass Jewel) Smallest butterfly in eastern Arabia and a local species, occurring in the Tuwayq Hills (April – November) and Qatar (all year). Habitat limited; often restricted to a single plant of the foodplant, *Heliotropium*. Male and female look similar. Has short, fast flight and often lands on stones on the wadi floor.

Nymphalidae (Tortoiseshells and Fritillaries)

Butterflies in this family are colourful, often common and have powerful flight. Front pair of legs small and cannot be used; butterfly relies on the other 2 pairs for walking.

FEBRUARY – APRIL

***Melitaea persea* Kollar** (Persian Fritillary) This species has a different life-cycle from any other species of butterfly in eastern Arabia. It passes summer, autumn and winter as a tiny larva in hibernation at the base of the larval foodplant, *Teucrium oliverianum* (Desert Germander), a herb used by The Bedouin to flavour their tea. In the spring many wadis are carpeted with the blue flowers which are visited by large numbers of *M. persea*. The Saudi Arabian sub-species is only found in the Tuwayq Hills; it differs considerably from the Iraq and Persian butterflies in diminished size and number of black spots on the upperside of the wings.

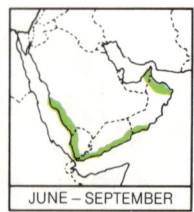

JUNE – SEPTEMBER

***Hypolimnas misippus* Linnaeus** (Diadem) Common name 'Diadem' derived from coloration of male, with its distinctive white spots and purple hue. Female differs completely and is an interesting example of mimicry. On first inspection, it could be mistaken for *Danaus chrysippus* (Plain Tiger or Lesser Wanderer), also illustrated. This provides a degree of protection as most birds and lizards will not touch any butterfly that is likely to have the unpleasant taste of *D. chrysippus*. To date only found in gardens and oases of northern Oman even though *Portulaca*, foodplant of the larva, is widespread. This suggests that the restricted range is due to climatic limitations.

Faisal's Pinnacle, Central Saudi Arabia

underside

underside

Teucrium oliverianum

underside

♀   ♂

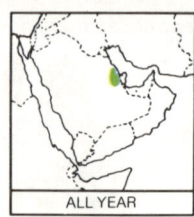
ALL YEAR

***Junonia orithya cheesmani* Riley** (Blue Pansy) Two subspecies of this widely distributed butterfly are found in Arabia. Subspecies *cheesmani* does not normally migrate and is confined to Al Hasa, Qatif Oasis, Tarut Island and Bahrain. The butterfly can be found in considerable numbers in date palm plantations. When disturbed will fly short distances rapidly but then returns to original area. Butterflies are attracted to flowers of alfalfa, but larval foodplants are *Convolvulus* and *Lippia*.

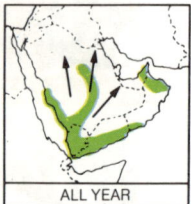
ALL YEAR

***Junonia orithya here* Lang** (Blue Pansy) This subspecies migrates and is found throughout most of the area. Male is distinguished from male of subspecies *cheesmani* by markings on forewing. Subspecies *here* have 2 white bars at tip of each forewing, whereas subspecies *cheesmani* males have 1 blue and 1 white. In all other respects the two subspecies are similar. Males are pugnacious towards intruders within their territory. Both sexes can be found feeding on the ground on fallen dates. Foodplants *Convolvulus* and *Lippia*.

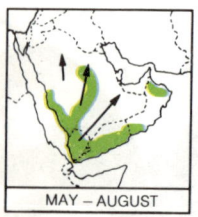
MAY — AUGUST

***Junonia hierta* Fabricius** (Yellow Pansy) Until recently only been found near Abha and Taif in the west of Saudi Arabia and at the Jabal Akhdar in northern Oman. During spring 1983, D. H. Walker and A. J. Walker discovered a thriving colony in the Tuwayq Hills, at Al Ghat in Saudi Arabia. Fond of mountainous country where it frequents wadis and argricultural land. Foodplants are various Acanthaceae.

NOVEMBER – MAY

***Vanessa cardui* Linnaeus** (Painted Lady) This noted migrant is one of the world's most widespread butterflies and is found throughout Arabia. However, it only breeds in certain selected localities where the larval food is common. Foodplants are *Urtica*, *Forskohlea*, *Malva* and *Neurada procumbens* (Creeping Thorn Rose). Larvae initially hide in tents of leaves which they tie together with silk, but when they are abundant it is common to see large numbers on the ground proceeding *en masse* to fresh foodplants. This often occurs in the steppe areas of eastern Saudi Arabia to the north and west of Manifa. The butterflies are found in large numbers on flowers of *Lycium shawi*, *Lantana* and *Tagetes* spp. (African Marigold) during March and April, before they migrate north.

Satyridae (Brown Butterflies)

MARCH – AUGUST

***Ypthima bolanica* Marshall** (Baluchi Ringlet) Found in hot, well-watered wadis of northern Oman which can support clumps of the foodplant, tussock grass. May also exist in eastern Saudi Arabia, where there are suitable habitats.

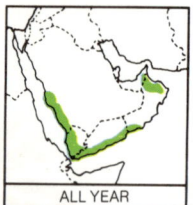

ALL YEAR

***Ypthima asterope* Klug** (African Ringlet) Common in western Arabia but to date only found in northern Oman. Not often seen, it inhabits date plantations and grassy hillsides where it spends long periods sitting on the ground; thus could easily have been overlooked in eastern Saudi Arabia where suitable localities exist. Foodplant is grass.

SPRING & AUTUMN

***Neohipparchia parisatis* Kollar** (White-edged Rock-Brown) Large, rather secretive and found only in ravines of the northern Omani Mountains, within the area covered by this book. However, could also occur in mountains of United Arab Emirates or in Saudi Arabia. Butterfly emerges from pupa in spring and then hibernates during heat of summer to reappear during autumn rains. During this season it breeds, thus enabling larvae to feed on the foodplant, grass, when it is plentiful.

ovum ×8

underside

Danaidae (Monarch Butterflies)

FEBRUARY – NOVEMBER

***Danaus chrysippus* Linnaeus** (Plain Tiger or Lesser Wanderer) One of the most conspicuous butterflies of Arabia and a strong migrant. Generally found in wadis and oases, wherever one of the 3 main foodplants of the larvae occur. These foodplants, *Calotropis procera* (Sodom's Apple), *Leptadenia pyrotechnica* (Fire Bush) and *Pergularia tomentosa* (Stranglevine), all belong to the milkweed family. When broken the plants exude a sticky, white fluid which is poisonous. The Bedouin use the fluid as a herbal treatment for heart ailments in much the same way as *Digitalis purpurea* (Foxglove) is used in Europe. Larvae feed on these plants and incorporate the poison into their bodies which renders them unpalatable to most animals. Their striking appearance would appear to act as a warning of their unpleasant taste. The bright blue green or beige pupa and the adults also have an unpleasant taste. In consequence they have few predators, which may account for the leisurely flight of the butterfly. Specimen illustrated is typical of the form found in Arabia; however, 2 other forms occasionally occur. In one, the forewing apical area is fawn; in the other, central areas of hindwing are white.

Calotropis procera

pupa

Diptera
(True Flies)

This is one of the largest orders of insects and contains approximately 70 000 known species. The size, shape and colour of individual species differ so extremely that it is sometimes difficult to appreciate any common relationship. All species undergo the complete metamorphosis of egg, larva, pupa and adult insect, although some species are viviparous and the development occurs within the body of the female which produces live larvae. The adult fly does not grow; growth only occurs in the larvae. True legs are not found on the larvae which are commonly known as maggots. They often feed upon decaying matter.

A large number of the species assist in the disposal of carrion, dung and other rotting materials, and occupy an important niche in the ecological chain. However, some species are a pest to farmers and cause extensive damage to root crops. Other species are parasites and a veterinary hazard to sheep, cattle and horses. The larvae of many species live in water and often have breathing tubes that reach to the surface to obtain air. These larvae and some pupae also have the ability to swim.

Most adult flies have compound eyes and also often 3 ocelli. All flies have mouths which are adapted to sucking. They are unable to bite, although they often are able to pierce membranous material to obtain food. Adult flies feed mainly on plant and other juices, although some species are parasites which feed on blood. A few species are without wings and are incapable of flight. The majority can fly and are capable of great manoeuvrability. All adult flies have 1 pair of wings. During evolution the character and shape of the second pair of wings changed until they have become small protrusions. These have a tiny knob on the extremity and are known as halteres. The halteres vibrate at the same frequency as the main wings and act as gyroscopes, providing stability in flight.

Adult flies cannot sting, but many are brightly coloured and mimic bees and wasps. Female mosquitoes and other similar species attack man by feeding on his blood. The amount of blood taken is infinitesimal and the physical damage caused by the fly is minute, but they are often carriers of disease which may be transmitted while feeding. Malaria, yellow fever, sleeping sickness, and other very serious illnesses are all examples of fly-transmitted diseases. Other types of flies that do not attack man directly may act as vectors in the transference of different species of deadly germs. These flies obtain food from a variety of sources. They can be attracted to raw sewage, where their mouthparts and limbs become contaminated, and later may visit food stores. In this way they aid the transference of germs that cause diseases such as cholera, typhoid and food poisoning. Although flies continue to be a carrier of disease, modern medicine and increased hygiene cure and prevent a number of these serious illnesses.

Diptera can be divided into three main suborders:

Nematocera	(Craneflies, Mosquitoes and Gnats).
Brachycera	(Horseflies, Clegs, Robberflies and Beeflies).
Cyclorrhapha	(Advanced Flies).

Nematocera (Craneflies, Mosquitoes and Gnats)
Culicidae (Mosquitoes and Gnats)

JANUARY – DECEMBER

***Culex pipiens* Linnaeus** (Common Mosquito) Adult males of this family suck nectar and plant sap, but females are blood suckers and have a sharp proboscis to pierce skin of the host. Females require a meal of blood before they are able to lay fertile eggs. There are a number of different species of mosquitoes in Arabia, but *C. pipiens* is the most common. Fortunately in Arabia it does not appear to be a carrier of human disease. Eggs are laid on surface of water which must contain a high portion of organic matter which larvae can use for food. Larvae swim by wriggling their bodies and are often seen hanging head down from the surface as the air duct is at the tail end of the body.

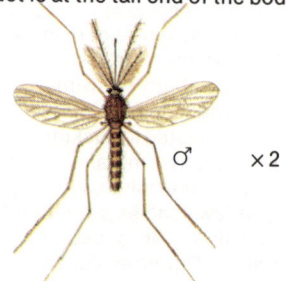

♂   × 2

JANUARY – NOVEMBER

***Anopheles* spp.** (Malaria Mosquitoes)   Capable of harbouring the malaria parasite which passes through a stage of its development in the mosquito. Malaria was widespread in the Hasa area, but the number of cases in Arabia during recent years has been greatly reduced. It is easier to identify *Anopheles* mosquitoes when they have settled. *Culex pipiens* (Common Mosquito) rests with body parallel to the surface on which it has settled, whereas the malaria mosquito rests with its body at an angle to the surface.

Chironomidae (Midges)

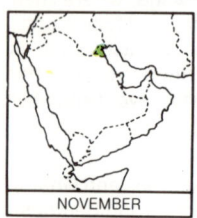

NOVEMBER

***Chironomus dorsalis* Meigen** (Green Midge)   Many members of this family resemble mosquitoes, but do not suck blood. Common around organically rich, stagnant water and sewage works. Larvae are aquatic and live off detritus deposits on the bottom of pools. Their bright red coloration is due to haemoglobin, a blood pigment.

× 1·5

Brachycera (Horseflies, Clegs, Robberflies and Beeflies)

Tabanidae (Horseflies and Clegs)

AUGUST

***Tabanus mordax* Austen** (Grey Gadfly) Adult males of this family feed off plant juices, but females suck blood. The females are particularly aggressive and can inflict a nasty wound. *Tabanus mordax* inhabits rock-strewn ravines, where the male generally spends hottest part of the day resting under rock ledges close to water. This species and the butterfly *Ypthima bolanica* (Baluchi Ringlet) are often found together.

♂ × 1.3

APRIL – AUGUST

***Tabanus rupinae* Austen** (Two-toned Horsefly) Inhabits oases and farms. Adult female is a pest of stabled livestock.

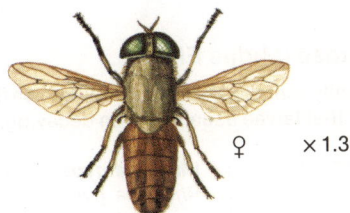
♀ × 1.3

APRIL – AUGUST

***Tabanus polygonus* Walker** (Grey Horsefly) Inhabits oases and farms. It is very similar to *T. rupinae*. (Not illustrated.)

Therevidae (Stiletto Flies)

***Hoplosathe frauenfeldi* Loew** (Masked Stiletto Fly) Frequents well-vegetated, temporary watercourses where the larvae live in damp soil. Adults often found around slaughterhouses.

×1·5

Conopidae (Thick-headed Flies)

***Conops nubeculipennis* Bezzi** (Hejaz Thickhead) Adult resembles a solitary wasp and can be found feeding off nectar from flowers in desert wadis and depressions. Larvae are internal parasites of solitary wasps.

×1·5

Mydaidae (Midas Flies)

This family contains the largest of all known flies. Little is known of their habits except that larvae usually live on decaying organic matter.

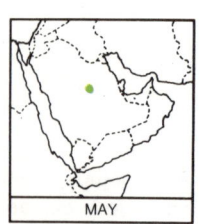

***Rhopalia gyps* Bowden sp.n.** (Walker's Midas Fly) *Rhopalia gyps* is a new species discovered in the Tuwayq Hills by D. H. Walker in 1980. In Appendix I, J. Bowden describes this insect for the first time.

×1·5

Asilidae (Robber Flies)

OCTOBER

***Apoclea femoralis* Wiedemann** (The Highwayman)
Flies in this family are fierce and active predators. They sit on a stone or branch waiting for a victim to pass, then fly out and seize it. Their legs are very strong and *A. femoralis* is capable of seizing large wasps or bees which it can carry off in flight. The prey is pierced with a sharp proboscis and sucked dry. Larvae feed on decaying organic matter.

× 1·5

Bombyliidae (Bee Flies)

FEBRUARY – APRIL

***Cytherea alexandrina* Becker** (Dusky Hoverer)
Many flies in this family resemble solitary wasps or bumble bees, but the flies only have 2 wings whereas bees have 4. *Cytherea alexandrina* inhabits small desert watercourses and wadis where it feeds off flowers. The eggs are laid near a solitary wasp or bee's nest. The young larva makes its way into the nest where it lives as a parasite.

× 1·5

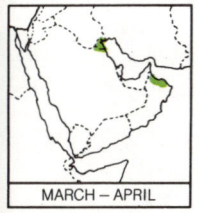

MARCH – APRIL

***Parachistus pulchellus* Greathead** (The Joker) Only discovered recently; full extent of its range is unknown. Frequents desert farms and likes borders of lucerne and radish fields. Male has not yet been found.

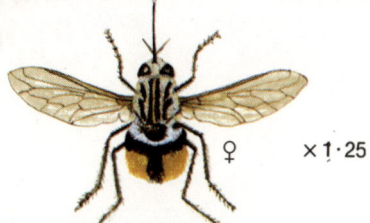

× 1·25

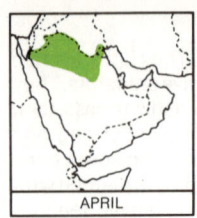

***Anastoechus trisignatus* Portschinsky** (Cowardly Bee Fly) Adult varies in colour, especially regarding extent of the yellow band on the body. Frequents rock-strewn areas of steppe which have plenty of *Rhanterium* plants, from which it feeds from the yellow flowers by hanging on blooms by 1 pair of legs.

Cyclorrhapha (Advanced Flies)
Drosophilidae (False Fruit Flies)

***Drosophila melanogaster* Meigen** (Vinegar Fly) Flies in this family live off fermenting organic matter, especially overripe fruit. In some species, larvae are parasites. *Drosophila melanogaster* is used extensively by biologists in the study of genetics because it breeds rapidly and has large chromosomes.

× 3

Tephritidae (True Fruit Flies)

***Dacus* (= *Leptoxyda*) *longistylus* Wiedemann** (Sodom's Apple Fruit Fly) Found on the plants of *Calotropis procera* (Sodom's Apple). During the hottest part of the day the flies rest under the leaves, but as temperatures drop they emerge to feed and court. Eggs laid in the soft green fruit or 'apple' of this poisonous plant.

× 2

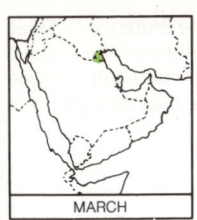

***Trupanea amoena* Frauenfeld** (Dusky Tip) Most larvae of this family feed in fruit and can be an orchard pest. *T. amoena* is common in low vegetation growing beside water in oases and farms. Dark markings on wings are thought to be associated with wing-fluttering used in courtship ritual.

 × 1.5

Ephydridae (Shoreflies)

***Ephydra flavipes* Macquart** (Pyrites Shorefly) The most common member of the family Ephydridae in Arabia. May be found around shoreline of most permanent bodies of water in oases and farms. The larva is aquatic and feeds on detritus.

 × 1.5

Syrphidae (Hoverflies)

There are a number of species of this family in Arabia and many are able to hover. They fly motionless in mid air until distracted, then move very rapidly in any direction. Often brightly coloured and may mimic wasps or bees. Larval food varies according to species and some are parasites.

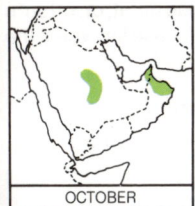

***Paragus compeditus* Wiedemann** (Glossy Hoverfly) *Paragus compeditus* is rare and found near water in gardens.

 × 1.5

***Metasyrphus luniger* Meigen** (Greater Tiger) One of the most common hoverflies in Arabia. Usually found in large numbers wherever vegetation occurs. Adults feed off nectar from flowers. Larvae carnivorous and generally eat aphids.

 × 1.5

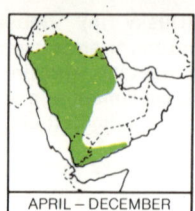

APRIL – DECEMBER

***Eristalinus aeneus* Scopoli** (Shiny Dronefly) Does not hover but spends most of the time on the ground. Often found in vicinity of slaughterhouses, sewage ponds and stagnant pools. Larvae feed on detritus in organically rich damp soils.

×2

×2

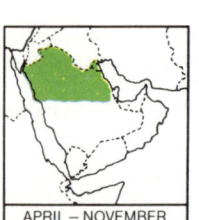

APRIL – NOVEMBER

***Eristalinus megacephalus* Rossi** (Big Headed Dronefly) Has similar habits to those of *Eristalinus aeneus* (Shiny Dronefly).

Calliphoridae (Bluebottles and Greenbottles)

Flies in this family frequent carrion, slaughterhouses, rubbish tips and other areas, where larvae feed on flesh.

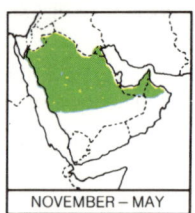

NOVEMBER – MAY

***Lucilia sericata* Meigen** (Winter Greenbottle) *Lucilia sericata* spends the hot summer months as pupa. Adult female lays eggs in dead meat, or, often in the wound of a live animal, in which case larvae eat the living flesh.

× 1.5

MARCH – JULY

***Wohlfahrtia nuba* Wiedemann** (Checkerspot Fly) Inhabits desert. Can be a nuisance to travellers, as it seeks moisture from the corner of the mouth or eye.

× 1.5

FEBRUARY – JUNE

***Chrysomya albiceps* Wiedemann** (False Greenbottle) Uncommon. Larvae eat larvae of other species of flies found in carrion and decaying matter. **A**

FEBRUARY – APRIL

***Chrysomya regalis* Robineau-Desvoidy** (Regal Bluebottle) Rare. Adults feed on animal juices, plant sap and honeydew. Larvae feed on carrion and faeces. **B**

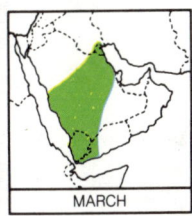

MARCH

***Sarcophaga ruficornis* Fabricius** (Rufous Fleshfly) Often seen sitting in the sun on the walls of houses. Larvae eat carrion and decaying matter. **C**

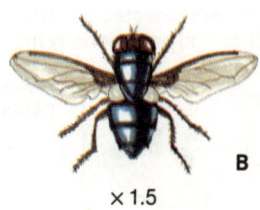

Muscidae (House-flies and others)

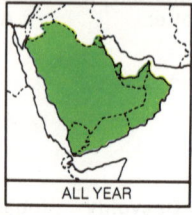
ALL YEAR

***Musca domestica* Linnaeus** (Housefly) The most universal fly and one of the most prolific. Probably one of man's worst pests. Although it does not attack man directly it is the vector for numerous diseases. Eggs are laid on a variety of substances, usually decomposing matter. Larvae develop rapidly, especially in a warm climate, and the whole life-cycle can be completed within 14 days. The fly moistens its food with saliva containing enzymes which prepare the food so that the fly can suck it up. This food may be putrid and contain germs. If the next meal is taken from a human food source, the regurgitated saliva will contain the germs from the fly's previous meal, thus creating a health hazard. This fly has followed man in his travels throughout the world and has no doubt helped to spread some of man's illnesses to remote areas.

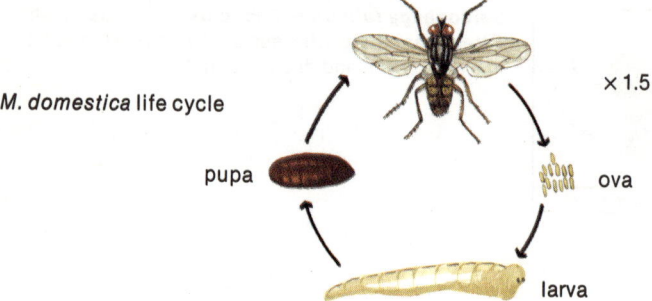

M. domestica life cycle — pupa, ova, larva — ×1.5

Hippoboscidae (Keds or Louseflies)

Flies in this family are generally parasites. Different species are usually parasites on different hosts. Many of the species are wingless, but have feet with well-adapted claws for clinging to the host. Hosts include camels, sheep, dogs and occasionally man.

APRIL — MAY

***Hippobosca longipennis* Fabricius** (Dog Ked) A parasite of dogs.

×1.5

Siphonaptera
(Fleas)

In Arabia there are many different species of the order Siphonaptera. The adults are all small, wingless insects that live as parasites mainly on mammals, from whom they suck blood for food. The body of a flea is very thin which enables it to travel with ease through the hair or fur of the host. It is not easily dislodged because it has claws on the feet and numerous hairs on the body. The adult insect is able to identify a new host by the heat radiated from the body of the host and will decide upon its suitability after taking a sample meal of blood. The flea is able to join a host by jumping, and is capable of spectacular leaps which sometimes exceed 100 times the length of its own body.

In order to breed, a flea requires the correct host and a stable environment. A nomadic animal is unsuitable. Female fleas require a meal of blood before they are capable of laying eggs. These are sticky and are generally laid in or around the nest of the host and hatch within 2 weeks. Larvae have no legs or eyes, but have biting jaws and feed on detritus and the faeces of the adults, which often contain partially digested blood from the host. When fully grown the larvae pupate and remain in this state until disturbed. A disturbance which initiates the hatching of the adult fleas. Since the disturbance is usually caused by the return of the nest's owner, this ensures that new adult fleas have a host.

Many diseases are spread by fleas including the dreaded plague, which in the past has caused at least 30 million human deaths in Europe. This disease is transmitted to man by *Xenopsylla cheopis* (Rat Flea) from infected rodents. It is still present in Kuwait.

Pulicidae (Spiny Legged Fleas)

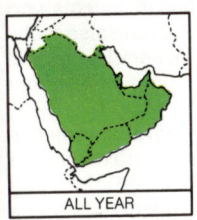

Pulex irritans Linnaeus (Human Flea) Common throughout the world, especially in many old-established towns where traditional ways of life have not changed. Can transmit infectious diseases. The natural hosts are foxes, not humans.

×6

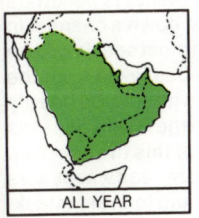

Ctenocephalides canis Curtis (Dog Flea) Found throughout the world on dogs, on which it can be present in large numbers. Excessive scratching by the dog often indicates presence of fleas. Eradication can be successful by dusting the dog and its basket with a proprietary flea powder. Less common than the Cat Flea.

×6

Hymenoptera
(Bees, Wasps, Ants and Ichneumon Wasps)

The Hymenoptera is one of the largest orders of insects and includes many highly developed species with specialized patterns of behaviour. They all undergo a full metamorphosis during their life-cycle. Most of the adult insects have compound eyes, 3 ocelli, biting mouths and 2 pairs of clear membranous wings. These wings are linked together during flight by small hooks. The name Hymenoptera is derived from two Greek words meaning 'membrane' and 'wing'. Most species have apodous larvae which are legless and have small heads. This form of larvae has evolved because it no longer has the necessity to search for food. The order is divided into two suborders, Symphyta (Sawflies) and Apocrita (Bees, Wasps, Ants and Ichneumon Wasps). Species belonging to the Symphyta are not covered by this book and are very rare in Arabia.

The adult Apocrita have the thorax and the first segment of the abdomen fused together. They are easily identified by a narrow 'waist' that exists between the first and second segment of the abdomen. The Symphyta do not have this narrow 'wasp' waist. The Apocrita is divided into two sections: the Aculeata (Bees, Wasps and Ants) and the Parasitica (Ichneumon Wasps). The insects of both sections provide their young (larvae) with food. The Aculeata include a large number of species that exhibit true social behaviour; apart from the Isoptera (Termites) they are the only insects to have reached this advanced stage of development.

The Aculeata have developed a symbiotic relationship with plants. In the primeval forests all plants were green, but during evolution plants developed flowers to contain their reproductive organs. These flowers have colour and scent which often can be recognized only by certain species of insects. Flowers also produce a surplus of nectar, an attractive food for insects who are guided to it by the pattern of the flower. Shapes of insects have also evolved, so that certain species can reach the nectar in certain flowers. During this foraging the insects generally pollinate or assist in the reproduction of the plant.

To deter predators most members of the Aculeata have developed means of defence. Bees and wasps are unpalatable because they have a tough skin which is usually covered in hairs. The ovipositor is often modified into a sting and connected to a poison sac. The venom is a complex mixture of various substances and there is no known antidote. Because the ovipositor is a female organ, only the females have the capacity to sting. The ovipositor is needle sharp and consists of 2 lancets and a casing or stylet. The lancets penetrate the skin of the victim and poison passes into the wound down a channel in the stylet. To assist penetration the lancets are barbed. In most species these barbs are small and the sting can be withdrawn for re-use, even from the toughest skin. The Honeybee is unable to successfully withdraw its heavily barbed sting from tough skins such as on humans. When the Honeybee tries to fly off it tears the sting out of its body and as a result of this the bee dies.

It is generally considered that the bright coloration of bees and wasps acts as a warning. This assists a predator to quickly identify and to avoid attacking an unpleasant prey. Certain species of ant are also unpleasant to taste and some have a sting or the capability of ejecting a jet of formic acid against attackers.

The Parasitica are all parasites. Generally they can be recognized by the long antennae which the insect moves continuously and by the forewings which usually contain a dark stigma. Eggs may be laid on a host, but in most species the female possesses a long ovipositor which is used to pierce the skin and to lay an egg in the living host. When the egg hatches the larva feeds on the host until it pupates. The host then dies. Larvae (caterpillars) of butterflies and moths are the most common host, but other insects are also attacked. Certain species of parasites are limited in their choice of acceptable food to particular hosts.

Parasites perform a useful function in controlling the size of host populations which otherwise could disrupt the ecological balance. In Arabia there are numerous species of parasites which include members of the families Evaniidae, Ichneumonidae and Braconidae. Their appearance and life-cycle vary, but broadly follows the pattern described above. Identification of individual species is beyond the scope of this book.

Sphecidae (Digger Wasps)

The family Sphecidae is the largest group of solitary wasps in Arabia. As the name implies they do not have a social behaviour. The queen is the only wasp to survive the winter and she establishes untended nests by digging tunnels into a soft bank of sand or earth.

MAY – SEPTEMBER

***Stizus vespoides* Walker** (Hornet Digger) The queen of *S. vespoides* digs several nests, but only lays 1 egg in each. She stocks each nest with grasshoppers she has paralysed with her sting, then blocks up the entrances after laying the single egg on the inert grasshoppers. The larva feeds on the live grasshoppers until it pupates. New wasps emerging from the pupae unblock the entrance to the nest and fly off in search of a mate. Adult insects are often seen flying around *Acacia* trees in search of nectar.

JUNE – AUGUST

***Stizus marnonis* Handlirsch** (Yellow Digger) Often seen flying around *Acacia* trees, but little is known of its life-history. It probably preys on either grasshoppers or praying mantises.

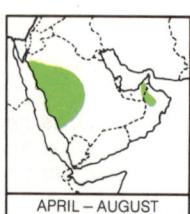

APRIL – AUGUST

***Stizus bizonatus* Spinola** (False Beetle Wasp) Often seen flying around *Acacia* trees; details of the life-history are unknown. This species and also *Scolia erythrocephala* (Red Headed Beetle Wasp) mimic the very aggressive *Vespa orientalis* (Oriental Wasp), which is a very good example of Müllerian mimicry. In 1878, Fritz Müller observed that several different species looked alike, even though they had no necessity to mimic as each had its own efficient defence mechanism. He considered the consequence of this mimicry to mean that a predator only had to learn the warning colour pattern once in order to avoid all the different species.

AUGUST

***Cerceris tricolorata* Spinola** (Ringed Digger) Visits low-growing flowers and is especially fond of *Heliotropium*. Constructs a nest in the ground and stocks it with small bees which it has paralysed.

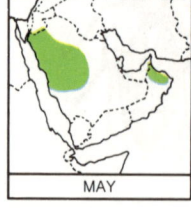

MAY

***Cerceris straminea* Dufour** (Black-tipped Digger) Uncommon and local. Occasionally attracted to herbaceous flowers.

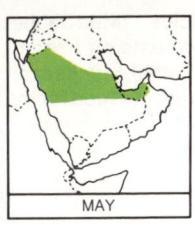

MAY

***Bembex dahlbomi* Handlirsch** (Olive Wasp Digger)
In Arabia there are a number of different species belonging to the genus *Bembex*. Their behaviour and appearance are similar. The wasps fly close to the ground near *Heliotropium* or *Pulicaria*. They dig shallow burrows for nests and these are stocked with small flies caught and paralysed on flowers.

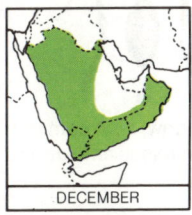

DECEMBER

***Philanthus triangulum* Fabricius** (Bee Wolf) Well known in southern Europe where it preys on the domesticated *Apis mellifera* (Honeybee) as well as various species of solitary bee. It builds a nest in the ground which it stocks with paralysed bees. Often dismembers its victims and feeds on honey contained in their crops.

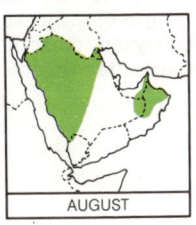

AUGUST

***Prionyx crudelis* Smith** (Locust Terror) In Africa packs of this large ferocious wasp follow locust swarms and prey on the weaker individuals. In Arabia, generally confines its attention to species of *Anacridium* and *Heteracris*. It is capable of flying with heavy grasshoppers to its nest.

***Sceliphron madraspatanum* Fabricius** (Mud Dauber Wasp) Constructs multi-celled nests on trees or rocks and uses mud as building material. Stocks each cell with paralysed spiders to provide live food for the larvae.

***Sphex fumicatus* Christ** (The Shadow) A common predator of grasshoppers found in oases and around *Acacia* trees.

***Parapsammophila turanica* Morawitz** (Cineraous Wasp) Builds the nest before finding its prey. Stocks completed brood burrow with paralysed, smooth-skinned caterpillars, lays egg and seals the entrance.

***Podalonia tydei* LeGuillou** (Common Sand Wasp) There are several species of *Podalonia* found in Arabia. Most are similar in appearance and behaviour to *P.tydei*. Stocks nest with hairless species of moth and butterfly larvae.

Scoliidae (Beetle Wasps)

***Scolia flavifrons* Fabricius** (Giant Beetle Wasp) The family Scoliidae includes some of the largest known species of Hymenoptera. For example, the wingspan of a female *S.flavifrons* can exceed 60 mm. The species are sexually dimorphic and larvae are parasites of various species of beetles. (Not illustrated.)

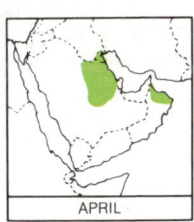

***Scolia erythrocephala* Fabricius** (Red Headed Beetle Wasp) Sexes are similar in appearance, but little is known of its life-cycle. There appears to be a case of Müllerian mimicry with the aggressive *Vespa orientalis* (Oriental Wasp).

***Campsomeriella thoracica* Fabricius** (Chafer Wasp) Sexes dimorphic. Male shows no resemblance to the female, as shown in the illustration. Habitat frequented by sexes is also different; males visit flowers, whereas females patrol areas of short grass and lawns. Female capable of detecting presence of Lawn Beetle larvae in their subterranean passages. It is not known how the wasp does this, but having located the beetle larvae she digs down and then lays an egg on the victim. The larva then develops ectoparasitically on the host.

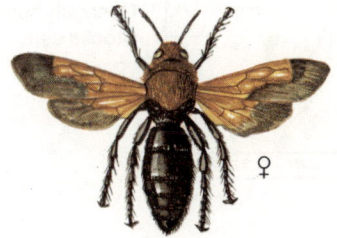

Eumenidae (Potter Wasps)

Wasps in this family construct nests from sand or mud mixed with saliva. Potter wasps mould this material to form ceramic nests, shaped like inverted urns, which are baked hard in the Arabian sun. These are hung singly from walls or rocks. Wasp lays one egg suspended from the roof of each nest after having filled it with paralysed prey. Mason wasps are similar, but use cavities between rocks or in the mortar of houses if this is soft. The nest is constructed with a number of cells, each for 1 occupant and each stocked with paralysed prey.

***Delta dimidiatipenne* Saussure** (Red Potter Wasp) The most common Arabian Potter Wasp. Female is often seen feeding from *Acacia* blossom or hovering around gardens in search of caterpillars to stock nests.

A

***Delta campaniforme* Fabricius** (Harlequin Potter Wasp) Favours oases and town gardens as habitat.

***Rhynchium oculatum* Fabricius** (Two-toned Mason Wasp) Little is known of the life-history.

***Euodynerus excellens* Perez** (Red Mason Wasp) Generally builds nest in hard banks of sand or soft rock. Stocks cells with paralysed caterpillars.

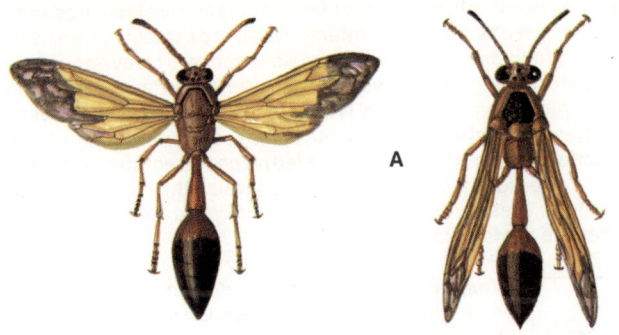
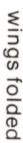

wings folded

A

A pool in the limestone escarpment of the Tuwayq Hills, Saudi Arabia

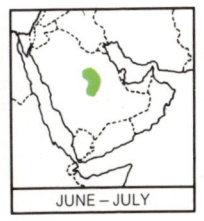

JUNE – JULY

***Chlorodynerus* spp.** (Yellow Mason Wasps) There are a number of species of the genus *Chlorodynerus*, all with similar habits. They make multi-celled nests and lay a single egg in each cell which is stocked with paralysed prey. Species of prey depend on species of wasp.

Vespidae (True Wasps)

Members of the Vespidae live in communal colonies and are known as social wasps. Only the queen survives the winter and in spring establishes a new colony. This colony includes queens whose main purpose is to lay eggs. It also includes males for mating. Female worker wasps generally forage for food and attend to construction and other jobs. Nest is made of paper which the wasps usually manufacture by chewing wood into pulp. Nest contains tiers of cells, each larva occupying a single cell. Larvae are fed pulped insects by the workers. Social wasps can be identified by the manner in which they fold their wings when not in flight. These are rolled up longitudinally and held at an angle to the body; they are not laid flat on the body.

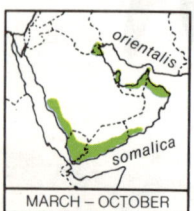
MARCH – OCTOBER

***Vespa orientalis* Linnaeus** (Oriental Wasp) Common wherever there is vegetation and insect life. It is a fierce predator. A single nest can contain several thousand wasps, and it is inadvisable to interfere with it unless special safety precautions are taken.

ssp. *orientalis*

APRIL – NOVEMBER

***Polistes wattii* Cameron** (Arabian Paper Wasp) Common and frequents oases, where it builds small nests which usually contain fewer than 50 cells. Nest is suspended, is made of paper and does not have a protective outer cover. During hot weather, wasps congregate at water, quench their thirst and carry a supply back to the larvae in the nest.

Pompilidae (Spider Hunting Wasps)

Wasps of the family Pompilidae are solitary. They have very long legs and are extremely agile. They hunt spiders, which they chase and paralyse by stinging. The wasp drags a paralysed spider to a suitable area, where it digs a burrow and places it within. Further paralysed spiders may be added before the wasp lays one egg and seals up the entrance.

***Cyphononyx bretonii* Guérin** (Spider Witch) Favours areas of sand and stone desert which have isolated clumps of vegetation.

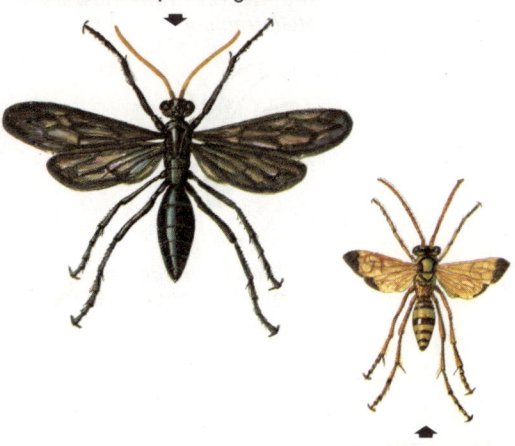

***Batozonellus fuliginosus* Klug** (Banded Spider Wasp) Adults are dimorphic. Male is illustrated. The female resembles *Cyphononyx bretonii* (Spider Witch) in shape, colour and behaviour and also frequents sand and stone deserts. Confusion of identification is unlikely, because the two species do not fly at the same time of year.

***Mygnimia dorsalis* Lepeletièr** (Orange Wings) Prefers shaded areas in oases, where it uses its wings, legs and antennae to locate and hunt spiders.

Chrysididae (Cuckoo Wasps)

***Chrysis ehrenbergi* Dahlbom** (Bronze Ruby Tail) There are several species of the family Chrysididae in Arabia, all brightly coloured and similar in habit to *C. ehrenbergi*. Does not make nest, but invades those of other species where it lays eggs in cells provided for the larvae of the host wasp. Larva of *C. ehrenbergi* initially feeds on the host's egg and pollen. Later, workers of host wasp feed the parasite. Adult often seen sipping nectar from flowers of *Ochradenus* and *Heliotropium*.

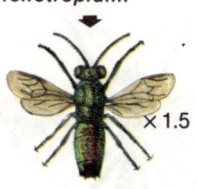

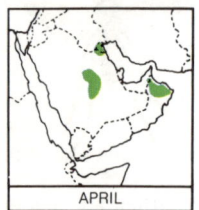

***Stilbum cyanurum* Forster** (Emerald Cuckoo Wasp) Common throughout Europe and the Middle East and fond of glades in woods, orchards and fringes of oases. During the heat of day, 4 or 5 insects may gather on one favourite plant.

Formicidae (Ants)

The Formicidae contains some of the most highly developed species of insects in the world. Only queens and the males have wings. They pair during a nuptial flight which occurs under favourable weather conditions when all winged ants take flight at the same time. Such flights may occur several times a year. After they land, the wings are discarded and the queen will either create a new colony or join an established one. The colonies are usually subterranean, although they may be in timber. Ants are able to chew wood, but they do not use it for food as most ants are predators on other insects.

There are several different castes of ant in each species. Generally only queens can lay eggs. Other female ants act as workers in the nest, where they may undertake construction work, fetch food or tend the young. Most species have a soldier caste which is usually stronger with well-developed mandibles and is capable of defending the nest. In some species another caste, called a replete, exists; these ants hang from nest roof and are fed honey, which they gorge. Their distended bodies are used as a living store to contain a reserve of food for the colony. Certain species raid other species and carry off the eggs; the ants that hatch are used as slaves in the nest.

A number of species tend various Homoptera, which they feed and may herd in underground chambers. These are usually milked for their 'honeydew'. Other species cultivate subterranean fields of fungi on specially prepared leaf litter. The fungi are cropped for food.

In Arabia there are a large number of different species of ant, but in this book there is only space to refer to 3.

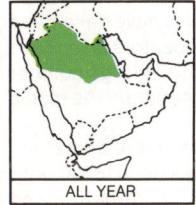

***Camponotus xerxes* Forel** (Desert Giant Ant) Probably the largest Arabian ant. Although nocturnal, it is often seen at dusk. Soldiers generally appear first, followed by the much smaller workers. The nest is usually found at the base of a wall or under a bush or tree.

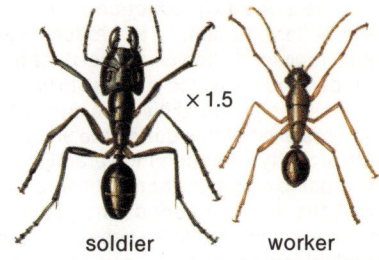

***Camponotus sericeus* Fabricius** (Golden Tailed Ant) Diurnal and often seen climbing herbaceous flowers or shrubs in search of nectar. Conspicuous when the sun's rays are reflected from the golden hairs of its abdomen.

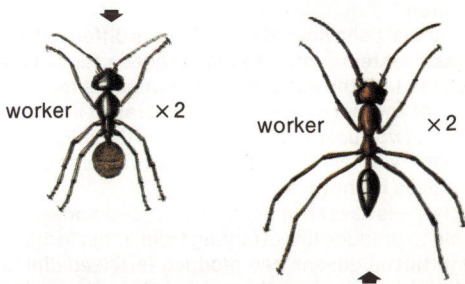

***Cataglyphis niger* André** (Desert Runner) Deserts with scattered shrubs and fringes of oases are favoured habitats. Generally moves quickly; solitary individuals often observed foraging some distance from nest. Colour varies in different colonies, but the ant can always be recognized by a laterally compressed abdomen held in a reflex position over the thorax.

Apoidea (Bees)

The super family Apoidea includes both social and solitary bees. There are approximately 20 000 known species in the world. The main difference between bees and wasps is their diet. Bees prefer nectar and pollen, whereas wasps are generally predators on other insects. The hairs on the body of a bee have branches and their arrangement assists in the collection of pollen whereas those on a wasp are smooth and lay flat. This difference in the shape of the hairs is a useful aid to identification. Bee mouthparts have developed so that the tongue can collect nectar from plants. Chemoreceptors at the base of the tongue permit the bee to taste and to select its food. A large number of species only reproduce by parthenogenesis and consequently the males of some species are extremely rare.

Some species of social bee, particularly *Apis mellifera* and *A. dorsatum*, are kept for the domestic production of honey. These bees need to eat both nectar and pollen in quantity to produce wax for nest construction and predigested food for the larvae. Some of the nectar is converted in the bee's body to produce honey which is stored in the nest for future use as food. For centuries man has provided hives as sites where bees can construct their nests. Records exist of this during the ancient Egyptian and Greek civilizations. Until recently it was common practice to kill the bees at the end of the season in order to obtain the honey. In nature, the queen and workers hibernate during the dormant period. The modern apiary includes permanent quarters (brood chambers) for the bees and separate, easily removed compartments (supers) for storing the honey. This system obviates the necessity to kill the bees. In Arabia, the honey bee is kept by some farmers not only for the supply of honey, but also for the pollination of crops.

It has been observed that bees start and finish their foraging at more or less regular times each day. This facility to judge the time and the ability to see a band of ultraviolet light in the sky gives the insect basic information for navigation.

The social behaviour of honeybees is different from that of wasps or ants. The caste system contains a female queen, female workers and male drones. The queen lays the eggs and only 1 queen is tolerated in each hive. The existence of another queen in a hive will result in either a fight to the death between the two queens or the partition of the colony. When the colony divides, one queen will leave with her followers in search of a new site. This congregation of bees is known as a swarm.'

Social bees have an unusual sexual condition known as haplodiploidy; they are able to produce live offspring from either fertilised or unfertilised eggs. Only fertilised queens can produce fertilised diploid eggs, which contain genetic information from the males and female and develop into females. Both fertilized and unfertilized queens (and also some female workers) can produce unfertilized haploid eggs. These contain genetic information only from the female and develop into males (or drones).

APRIL – AUGUST

***Xylocopa aestuans* Linnaeus** (Canary Carpenter Bee) *Xylocopa aestuans* is a species of solitary bee. Male and female differ in appearance, as illustrated. Common and often seen in gardens and oases. Builds nest of multi-celled tunnels in dead wood.

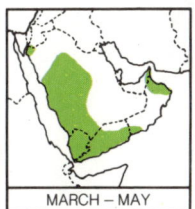

MARCH – MAY

***Xylocopa* spp.** (Carpenter Bees) There are several blackish species of the genus *Xylocopa* in Arabia. They favour scrub desert habitat and congregate at *Acacia* blossom, often driving away other bees.

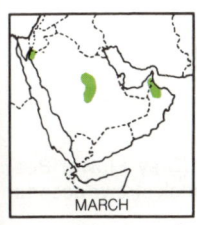

MARCH

***Paracrocisa sinaitica* Alfken** (Domino Bee) This rare species of solitary bee is found in wadis, whereas the closely related *Thyreus* bees (not included in this book) frequent gardens and oases. They have a tendency to fly in small parties of between 2 and 6 individuals; frequently seen resting together on bare twigs.

Amegilla nubica Lepeletièr (Nubian Flower Bee) A solitary bee that inhabits rock-strewn deserts, it is heard more often than seen. Rarely alights as it prefers to imbibe nectar from flowers while in flight. It can hover; the long tongue extracting nectar from the deep-throated flowers of *Lycium persicum* (Persian Tea plant) and *Astragalus spinosus* (Spiny Milk Vetch).

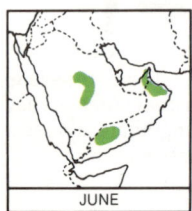

Amegilla byssina Klug (Blossom Bee) Often seen hovering around bushes of *Lycium*. It is a very fast flier.

Paramegilla semirufa Friese (Yellow Flower Bee) A solitary bee that inhabits rock-strewn deserts, where there are plenty of *Astragalus* or *Lycium* plants. It is active in evening.

Anthophora extricata Priesner (Grey Flower Bee) This solitary bee inhabits wadis in rock-strewn deserts.

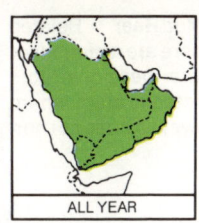

***Apis mellifera* Linnaeus** (Honey Bee) This and the Asiatic *A. dorsatum* (not included in this book) are the 2 main species of social bees kept for domestic production of honey.

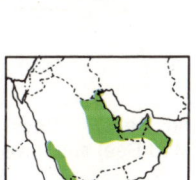

***Pseudapsis nilotica* Smith** (Zebra Bee) Common and found in oases and desert gardens where it is one of the most important pollinators of small flowers. Particularly attracted to *Ocimum*.

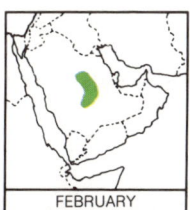

***Eucera dimidiata* Brullé** (Grey Longhorn Bee) Inhabits rock-strewn deserts where it frequents shallow water channels. Attracted to flowers of *Astragalus spinosus* (Spiny Milk Vetch) and *Heliotropium*. Appearance of the male is different from the female. Male has very long antennae which sweep back to the abdomen.

***Icteranthidium ferrugineum* Fabricius** (Wasp Bee)

***Chalicodoma rubripes* Morton** (Mud Bee) Related to the *Megachile* bees of which there are a number of species in Arabia. *Chalicodoma rubripes* constructs nest of mud, so its habitat is restricted to areas where fine soil and water are present. However, does not normally favour oases.

***Chalicodoma* spp.** (Lesser Mud Bees) Occasionally found with *C. rubripes* (Mud Bee) and have similar habits.

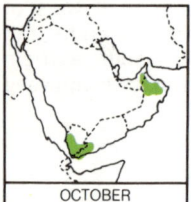

***Coelioxys afra* Lepeletièr** (Spiny-tailed Bee) Parasitic and solitary.

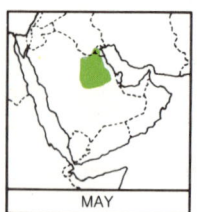

***Halictus seladonius* Lepeletièr** (Glossy Mining Bee) One of several species of the genus *Halictus* in Arabia. Most of them are small insects with few body hairs. They construct multi-celled nests by mining tunnels in light sandy soils which have been consolidated by recent rain. Some species are partially social and rear 1 brood of workers who assist in nest construction and attend to the larvae. In other species the queen never sees her offspring. They do not store food for the dormant season and only queens survive this period. The genus is often considered to be the link between solitary and social bees.

Coleoptera
(Beetles)

Beetles are one of the most successful forms of animal life found in the world today, with over 275 000 known species. Approximately one-quarter of all named species of animals in existence are beetles. Various types have evolved to take advantage of most available habitats and food sources. The order is divided into roughly 30 suborders which contain species that vary from some of the smallest to some of the largest known insects. The smallest beetles measure less than 0.3 mm in length, whereas the largest can be the size of a man's fist and weigh 110 g (4 oz). The life-cycle involves a full metamorphosis and includes egg, larva, pupa and adult stages. Most beetles can fly, but generally prefer to walk. The legs are normally well developed for walking, although in some cases they have been adapted for digging or swimming. The adult insect and some larvae have compound eyes, but very few possess ocelli. The antennae vary in length and shape according to the species, but are not always straight.

One of the main reasons for the success of beetles is their rugged exoskeleton which presents a creature that virtually lives inside a suit of armour. The forewings are made of rigid cuticle which fold down over the body and act as wing cases for the soft membranous hindwings, and at the same time protect the soft parts of the insect. These forewings are termed elytra and meet in a longitudinal line called the sulture which is on the upper surface of the beetle. The elytra and sulture are a characteristic of the order. A general hardening of the body cuticle for the remaining exposed surfaces completes the creature's defences.

This body formation presents a daunting target which can successfully withstand attack from a number of predators. However, the retention of body fluids is the most important advantage of its tough exterior. This prevents desiccation and allows the insect to survive in extremely dry environments. Water beetles also trap a reservoir of air in the space between the body and the elytra which allows them to stay under water for a considerable time.

Beetles have biting mouthparts and some species chew their food, which is often mixed with digestive juices. Other species suck liquids. All forms of organic material constitute a potential food source. These include trees, plants, insects, carrion and excreta, with different species being attracted to each type of food. Beetles carry out several useful functions: some act as pollinators, others are predators of plant pests such as aphids and yet others help to dispose of carrion. Some species are notorious as pests, causing extensive damage to crops and to the timber in properties.

Carabidae (Ground Beetles)

Beetles in the family Carabidae are all active predators which eat other beetles, woodlice, worms, caterpillars and small insects. They spend most of the time on the ground and are able to run. The majority of species are nocturnal and thus inactive during the day. Elytra are fused together on some species, which renders them incapable of flight, although it also affords extra protection.

FEBRUARY – MAY

Anthia duodecimguttata Bonelli (Domino Beetle) Inhabits areas of hard sand and rock where it hunts other insects and in particular the family Tenebrionidae (Darkling Beetles). Its own defence mechanism is an unpleasant smell which makes it unattractive to predators.

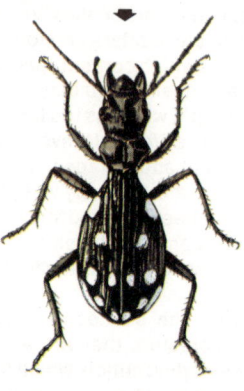

FEBRUARY – APRIL

Graphipterus minutus Dejean (Ant Domino) A ferocious diurnal predator whose main food source is ants. It is not unusual to find specimens that have 3 or 4 ants' heads still adhering to parts of their bodies. Prefers a habitat of rock-strewn desert plains with sparse vegetation.

Scarites guineensis Dejean (Sabre-toothed Beetle) A number of similar beetles of the genus *Scarites* are found in Arabia. *Scarites guineensis* is nocturnal.

JANUARY – MAY

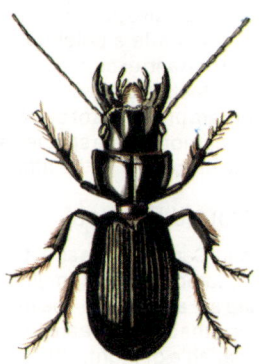

AUGUST

***Bembidion saxatile* Gyllenhal** (Brilliant Ground Beetle) Common throughout the Middle East and Europe, where it can generally be found in damp hollows or near water. Nocturnal, spending most daylight hours under stones or debris.

×2

JULY

***Chlaenius canariensis* Dejean** (Metallic Ground Beetle) Nearly all Arabian species of the genus *Chlaenius* have some gold coloration bordering the elytra. *Chlaenius canariensis* is distinguished by black elytra and a metallic green thorax. Nocturnal, spending the day beneath a stone or within a hole in the ground.

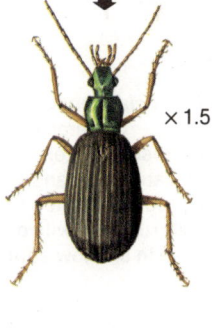
×1.5

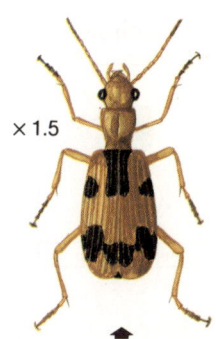
×1.5

JANUARY – JUNE

***Brachinus nobilis* Dejean** (Rufous Bombardier Beetle) Often found close to permanent pools and water tanks in areas of rock, sand and clay. Larvae and adults generally feed on other insects. A highly sophisticated method of defence has evolved internally within the adult. A cavity in the abdomen acts as a storage tank which leads into a chamber with a funnel-shaped exit at the beetle's rear. When threatened, the tank fills with 2 different body chemicals. Some of the mixture is supplied to the chamber, where it mixes with another substance creating a highly volatile mixture. An explosion occurs and the boiling mixture is fired out of the funnel which temporarily blinds the attacker and gives the beetle time to escape. The tank contains sufficient mixture for several successive explosions.

MARCH – MAY

***Calosoma imbricatum* Klug** (Beaded Runner)
Several species of *Calosoma* occur in Arabia, although *C. imbricatum* is the most common. Usual habitat is areas of rock-strewn plain with some vegetation. Hides during the day and starts to hunt at dusk, feeding on caterpillars, wood lice and other small creatures. This species is a strong nocturnal flier, although some of the other species are unable to fly.

Cicindelidae (Tiger Beetles)

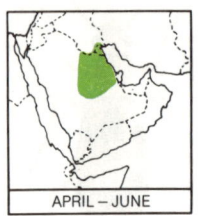

APRIL – JUNE

***Myriochile melancholica* Fabricius** (Melancholic Tiger Beetle) Generally found on open stretches of hard sand close to water. Frequents seashores, salt-flats, freshwater pools and streams. Adults and larvae are fierce predators which feed on other insects. The adult usually runs, but will readily take to flight. Larvae normally live in shallow subterranean burrows.

× 1.5

Dytiscidae (Diving Beetles)

Both this family and Hydrophilidae (Water Beetles) require an aquatic habitat. Although vast areas of Arabia are dry and hot there are a number of permanent pools of water. These permit the survival of many species. Migration often occurs to temporary pools if rain falls.

JUNE – AUGUST

Guignotus major Sharp (Miniature Diving Beetle) Common and found in good numbers in permanent pools and in temporary ponds. Both larvae and adults are fierce predators and often attack creatures many times their own size.

 ×2·5

ALL YEAR

Laccophilus pictipennis Sharp (Mottled Diving Beetle) Prefers permanent pools with plenty of water vegetation and algae.

 ×2·5

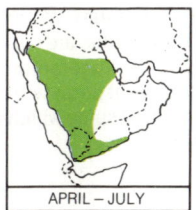
APRIL – JULY

Hyphydrus pictus Klug (Diving Pill) All diving beetles have streamlined profiles which permit them to move quickly through water. Legs are broad and hairy and act as efficient paddles. *Hyphydrus pictus* is particularly well adapted for swimming.

 ×2·5

APRIL – SEPTEMBER

Cybister tripunctatus Olivier (Short Legged Diving Beetle) Common and inhabits pools, reservoirs, rivers and irrigation ditches where reeds grow.

Eretes sticticus Linnaeus (Fawn Diving Beetle) The most common Diving Beetle in Arabia and attracted by any body of water, even chlorinated swimming pools. Equally at home in air or under water. Swarms come to lights during dispersal flights.

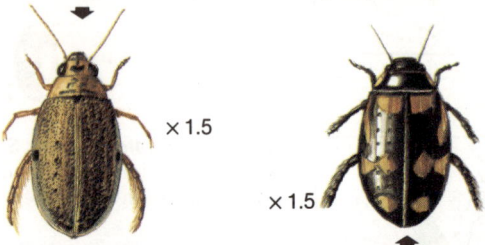

Prodaticus pictus Sharp (Polkadot Diving Beetle) Rare and only reported from 2 semi-permanent pools to date, although it is common in western Arabia.

Hydrophilidae (Water Beetles)

Hydrous mesopotamiae Knisch (Platinum Water Beetle) Larvae of the family Hydrophilidae are carnivorous, although adults are strictly vegetarian. Hydrous mesopotamiae prefers permanent pools with plenty of vegetation. The adult has a ventral spine which is very sharp and can inflict a nasty wound.

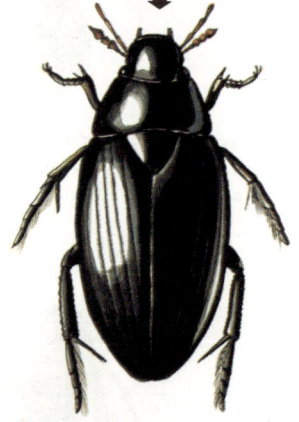

Hydrophilus aculeatus Solier (Spiny Tail) More common than Hydrous mesopotamiae (Platinum Water Beetle), although both have similar habits and the same habitat. Hydrophilus aculeatus can be identified by the elytra tips.

Nitidulidae (Sap-feeding Beetles)

MARCH – APRIL

***Nitidula ciliata* Erichson** (Carrion Beetle) Most species in the Nitidulidae feed on sap oozing from rotting plant material, or on fungi. *Nitidula ciliata* prefers carrion where it is usually found in the company of *Dermestes lardarius* (Larder Beetle) and *D. frischii* (Carcass Beetle). Distinguished by its light colour and the abdomen, which protrudes beyond the elytra.

 ×3

Meloidae (Oil Beetles)

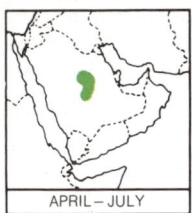

APRIL – JULY

***Nemognatha chrysomelina* Fabricius** (Bloodied Oil Beetle) Beetles in the family Meloidae, such as *N. chrysomelina*, differ from all others because of their parasitic habits. Eggs are laid in soil over a large area. After they hatch, the active larvae try to attach themselves to a host, usually a grasshopper. The beetle larva feeds on the eggs of the grasshopper after they have been deposited. Adults are clumsy fliers, and spend hours feeding in flower heads. If disturbed, beetle exudes globules of oil or blood from various joints as a defence. On sensitive skins this oil is a strong irritant.

 ×2    ×2

MARCH – APRIL

***Mylabris gratiosa* Marseul** (Leopard Oil Beetle) Meloidae, such as *M. gratiosa*, have distinctive shapes and are often brightly coloured. It is thought that this ensures predators easily recognise an insect that is likely to be unpalatable and thereby leave it alone.

***Croscherichia richteri* Kaszab** (Wasp Oil Beetle) Prefers desert steppe. Markings and colour vary considerably according to locality.

Coccinellidae (Ladybird Beetles)

***Henosepilachna elaterii* Rossi** (Eyed Ladybird) Vegetarian, feeding on surface tissue of leaves. Many plants act as hosts, but members of the cucumber family are preferred. As a vegetarian, *H. elaterii* is an unusual member of the family Coccinellidae since most species are predators during larval and adult stages.

***Coccinella undecimpunctata* Linnaeus** (Eleven-spot Ladybird) Prefers cultivated areas and gardens, where it feeds on aphids. Spots vary in size and number. The bright colours of the Coccinellidae warn predators of their bitter taste. If attacked, they exude droplets of pungent blood which is sufficient to deter most vertebrate predators.

***Coccinella septempunctata* Linnaeus** (Seven-spot Ladybird) The most common and widespread ladybird in Arabia. This species varies little in appearance.

Adonia variegata Goeze - (Variegated Ladybird) Wadis and fringes of oases are localities generally frequented. A great deal of variation occurs in colours, size and number of spots, which sometimes coalesce to form black bars.

Curculionidae (Weevils)

Ammocleonus aschabadensis Faust (Pinstriped Ground Weevil) Common at oases fringes and saltflats. Most Curculionidae feed on vegetation and possess a rostrum with jaws situated at the extremity which is used to bore into plant tissues. *Ammocleonus aschabadensis* is well protected by a very hard cuticle and good camouflage. Usually found on the ground, but often feeds on low bushes of *Zygophyllum*. When attacked, rolls over and lashes out with its feet which are armed with sharp claws.

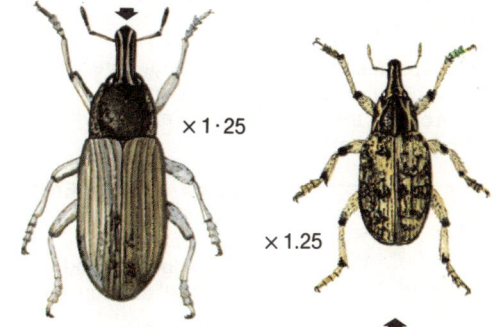

Bothynoderes anxius Gyllenhal (Elegant Ground Weevil) There are several similar species of the genus *Bothynoderes* in Arabia and all live on the ground. *Bothynoderes anxius* frequents farms and depressions in the desert that contain the plant *Salsola*.

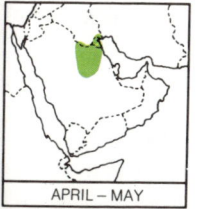

Sitophilus granarius Linnaeus (Grain Weevil) One of the most destructive pests in Arabia, it is not a native but has been imported and can be found in warehouses, granaries, flourmills and shops. Larvae bore into grain and eat the centre, leaving a hollow husk.

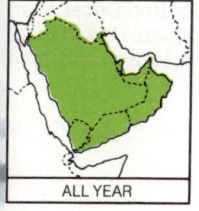

Elateridae (Click Beetles)

FEBRUARY – OCTOBER

Aeoloides grisescens Germar (Orange Legged Skip Jack)   There are several species of the family Elateridae in Arabia and *A. grisescens* is the most common, although the largest is *Lanelater notodonata* (not included in this book) which is 35 mm in length. During evolution this beetle has acquired an unusual ability to turn over. When it lands on its back, with legs in the air, it would appear to be at the mercy of any predator or likely to die of starvation. However, it is able to flick itself high into the air, rolling over in flight so that it lands on its feet. This stratagem is accompanied by a click, which is how this group acquired their common name. Larvae live in soil on roots of plants; they are pests and known as 'wireworms'. Adults feed on pollen and nectar of flowers.

× 2

Histeridae (Hister Beetles)

Most species in the family Histeridae are scavengers, feeding on dung, rotting vegetation, carrion and small insects. Generally shiny black or black and red in colour, they have a very hard exterior with truncated elytra which exposes 2 body segments.

MARCH – APRIL

Saprinus ornatus Erichson (Ornate Undertaker) *Saprinus ornatus* is uncommon and lives in open stone-strewn desert, where it feeds on carcasses of small birds, hedgehogs and rodents. Larvae are predators of other small creatures.

× 2

JANUARY – APRIL

Saprinus uvarovi Müller (Red Spotted Undertaker) Has similar habits to *S. ornatus* (Ornate Undertaker). Both species can withdraw legs flat to body and feign death when attacked.

× 2

Cleridae (Checkered Beetles)

FEBRUARY – MAY

***Necrobia rufipes* de Geer** (Copra Beetle) Feeds on carrion and stored meat and can be a pest. The adult is covered in minute hairs. Common throughout the area where it can be found under decaying sheep, goats or camels. When disturbed it runs very fast and will try to hide. Avoids bright sunlight.

 ×2

Dermestidae (Hide or Carpet Beetles)

AUGUST – SEPTEMBER

***Anthrenus flavipes* Leconte** (Gaudy Carpet Beetle) Although found on dried carcasses and in birds' nests and animal lairs, it is now very common in domestic habitations. Larvae cause extensive damage to carpets, furs and other garments. The larvae are covered in long hairs and have been given the name 'woolly bears'.

 ×4.5

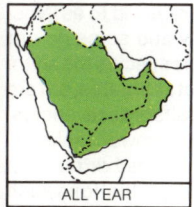

ALL YEAR

***Dermestes lardarius* Linnaeus** (Larder Beetle) Common in meat stores and curriers, it can be found in the wild on dried carcasses. The hairy larvae are often found scurrying about with other larvae such as those of Calliphorid flies (Bluebottles and Greenbott'

 underside

JANUARY – JUNE

***Dermestes frischii* Kugelmann** (Carcass Beetle) Very similar in appearance and habits to *D. lardarius* (Larder Beetle), this species has a white under-surface. On rare occasions it is found in meat stores, but is more common on sheep, goat and camel carcasses in the desert. Performs a useful function assisting in the disposal of dead animals. When disturbed, adults feign death and withdraw legs into grooves on underside of the body.

Silvanidae (Toothed Beetles)

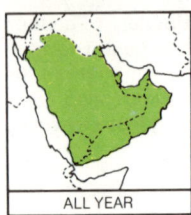
ALL YEAR

***Oryzaephilus mercator* Fauvel** (Merchant Grain Beetle) Seldom found outside granaries and shops, it is a scavenger which feeds mainly on stored food products.

 × 3

Bruchidae (Pea Beetles)

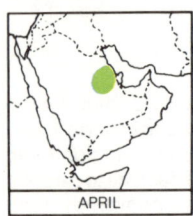
APRIL

***Callosobruchus maculatus* Fabricius** (Spotted Bean Weevil) Many different species of this genus probably occur in Arabia. In most cases, the larvae develop inside seed pods of the legume family. Other members of the Bruchidae infest stored peas, beans and lentils.

 × 4

Tenebrionidae (Darkling Beetles)

The Tenebrionidae is the largest family of beetles, often referred to as 'Nocturnal Ground Beetles'. They are generally unable to fly and some do not possess wings. Adults are either black or brown and in some species the elytra are fused together. The insects are uncommon in temperate climates, but are numerous in the dry, hot deserts of the world. Larvae and adults are scavengers, living among dried plant material, often in the food stores or burrows of animals. The insects have the ability to manufacture all the water they need within their bodies metabolically, which permits them to live in very dry situations such as man's flour stores.

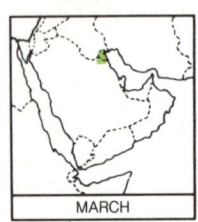
MARCH

***Micipsa* spp.**
Micipsa includes a number of species found in Arabia, all of which look similar to the beetle illustrated.

 × 1.5

JANUARY – OCTOBER

***Opatroides punctulatus* Brullé**   (Fake Flour Beetle) Found beneath stones and logs close to human habitation. Distinguished from small species of *Tenebrio* (Flour Beetles) by a row of indentations present on the elytra.

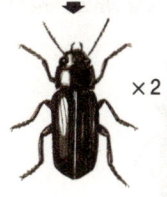

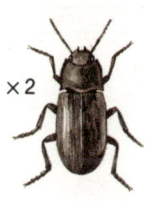

JANUARY – APRIL

***Opatropsis hispida* Brullé**   (Hispid Beetle)   Uncommon nocturnal beetle found in animal burrows.

***Pimelia arabica* Klug**   (Arabian Darkling Beetle) One of the most common species of Arabia and found in most localities. There are several similar species in the genus *Pimelia*. *Pimelia arabica* is distinguished by rows of protrusions on the elytra which are surmounted by hairs.

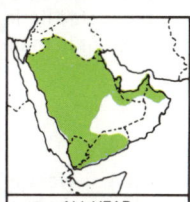

ALL YEAR

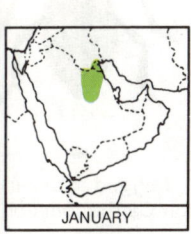

JANUARY

***Pimelia* spp.**   (Darkling Beetles)   Numerous *Pimelia* inhabit the rocky areas of Saudi Arabia in a bewildering variety of species.

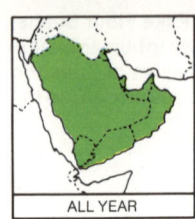

ALL YEAR

***Tenebrio molitor* Linnaeus** (Flour Beetle) Originally, its habitat was confined to food stored in burrows of certain species of rodents. However, *T. molitor* has spread to human dwellings and is now common where flour and cereal products are stored. Larvae are pests and known as 'mealy worms'.

× 1.25

× 5

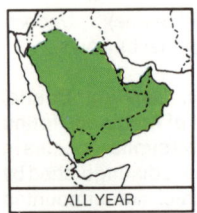

ALL YEAR

***Tribolium castaneum* Herbst** (Rust Red Flour Beetle) This species and *T. confusum* (not included in this book) are similar and do not appear to be natives of Arabia. However they are found in contaminated flour, biscuits and other dried cereals. Only occur in man-made environments.

MARCH – AUGUST

***Ocnera hispida* Forskål** (Scarce Stalker) Nocturnal and prefers the neighbourhood of human habitation. Feeds off litter and excrement.

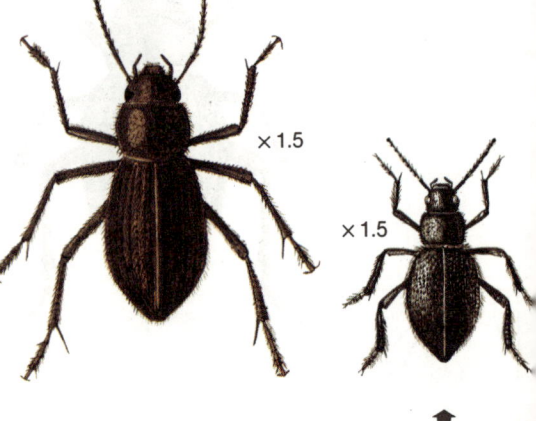

× 1.5   × 1.5

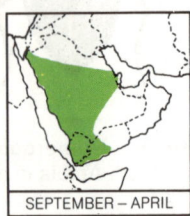

SEPTEMBER – APRIL

***Thriptera crinita* Klug** (Short Legged Stalker) Favours areas of rock and vegetation. Can be common in town suburbs.

SEPTEMBER – APRIL

***Blaps kollari* Seidlitz** (Churchyard Beetle) A number of similar species of *Blaps* occur in Arabia and generally frequent rock outcrops close to human habitation. They have strictly nocturnal habits. Adult has an opening in the vicinity of the anal projections from which it can discharge a jet of foul-smelling liquid at an attacker.

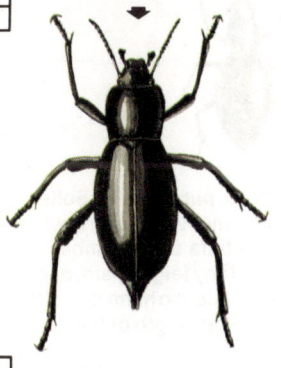

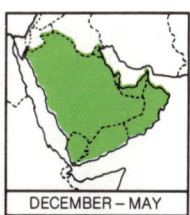

DECEMBER – MAY

***Adesmia cancellata* Klug** (Pitted Beetle) Common throughout Arabia, it can be found wherever there is vegetation. Feeds off organic debris from plants, including seeds, scraps of fruit, flowers and dead plants. Active during the day and uses its long legs to lift its body well clear of the hot ground. The insect increases the clearance as the temperature rises.

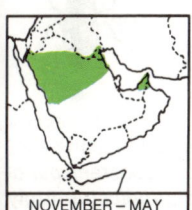

NOVEMBER – MAY

***Adesmia stoeckleini* Koch** (Elevated Stalker) Prefers firm ground with plenty of vegetation. In northeastern areas almost entirely replaced by the very similar *A. aenescens* (not included in this book). Both species are active during the day.

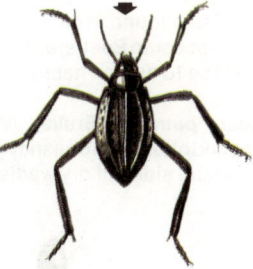

NOVEMBER – MAY

***Adesmia cothurnata* Forskål** (Variable Stalker) Uncommon and inhabits stone deserts.

FEBRUARY–DECEMBER

***Tentyrina palmeri* Crotch** (Rack Beetle)   Several similar species of the genera *Tentyrina* and *Mesostena* occur in Arabia, but *T. palmeri* is the most common. Nocturnal scavengers, generally living in close proximity to human habitation.

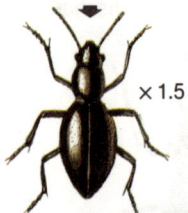
×1.5

×1.5

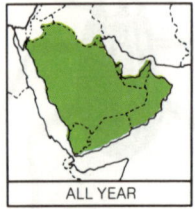

ALL YEAR

***Mesostena puncticollis* Solier**   (Opossum Beetle) One of the most common beetles in Arabia. Found in good numbers under timber during the day. When disturbed they feign death, opossum fashion. It is extremely difficult to harm one of these beetles because of the great strength of the cuticle.

***Paraplatyope arabica* Blair**   (Savile Row Beetle) Scarce and nocturnal. Inhabits outcrops of rock.

JANUARY – MARCH

×2

***Oxycara* spp.**   (Pellet Beetles)   There are several similar species of the genus *Oxycara* found in Saudi Arabia. Often found in company of *Mesostena puncticollis* (Opossum Beetle) and *Scleron sulcatum* (Ugly Trox), close to human habitation.

MARCH – MAY

***Zophosis punctata* Brullé**   (Whizz Beetle)   Fast moving and often seen on sandy ground in desert farms. Also favours sides of dry wadis.

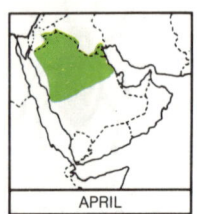

APRIL

×1.5

Zophosis complanata Solier (Sand Swimmer) Normally found in sand dunes. Exterior exceptionally smooth enabling it to 'swim' in sand. Often detected moving rapidly through sand just below the surface. Some specimens covered with fine orange or light-green powder which easily rubs off; this can lead to false identification.

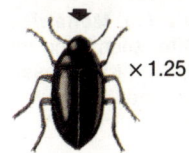

× 1.25

Erodius octocostatus Peyerimhoff (Giant Sand Swimmer) After heavy rains in the desert, many can be seen pairing on sand dunes. Capable of 'swimming' in sand, they spend the time permanently in this environment, where they feed off wind-blown seeds and other wind-borne debris. There are several similar species of the genus *Erodius* in Arabia, but *E. octocostatus* is easily identified by 8 ribs on the elytra.

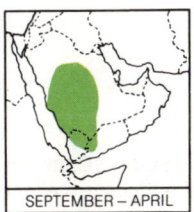

Scleron sulcatum Baudi *(Ugly Trox)* An inhabitant of rodent burrows in stony soil near farms and oases.

× 2

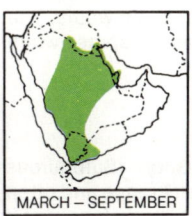

Prionotheca coronata Olivier (Urchin Beetle) Not common although occasionally found in open deserts close to human habitation. It has ferocious-looking lateral spines, but is quite harmless. Feeds on seeds, leaves, culinary vegetable waste and dead organic material. Nocturnal. (See p. 147.)

Buprestidae (Jewel Beetles)

Adults of the family Buprestidae generally have a shiny metallic and colourful appearance. Most larvae have soft bodies and bore into living trees. They tunnel into the pith of young shoots or just beneath the bark. Some species grow for many years before they mature and pupate. In Arabia many of the desert species prefer to develop in roots of trees where it is damper and cooler.

***Capnodis excisa* Ménétriès** (Desert Knotweed Beetle)   Often seen flying noisily around *Calligonum comosum* (Desert Knotgrass), a shrub which it finds especially attractive and which is common on many sand dunes.

***Steraspis speciosa* Klug** (Emerald Beetle)   Rare and the largest species of the genus *Steraspis* found in Arabia. Attracted to *Acacia* trees situated in rock-strewn deserts.

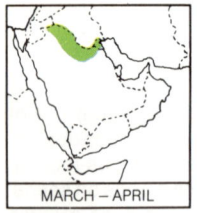

***Sphenoptera faragi* Thery** (Dusky Jewel)   Common within its habitat, but easily overlooked due to excellent camouflage. Often found in good numbers on the lower stems of *Astragalus spinosus* (Spiny Milk Vetch), a plant which generally grows in shallow wadis. The insect retreats into the plant's mass of spines when disturbed.

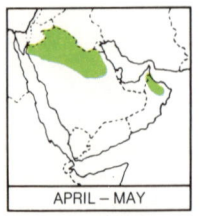

***Julodis euphratica* Castelnau and Gory** (Sulphurous Jewel Beetle)   Common within its range and often seen flying noisily around *Acacia* trees or feeding off the scented yellow flowers. Another very similar species *J. distincta* (not included in this book) replaces *J. euphratica* in north east Saudi Arabia and Kuwait. It has a coat of long, fine hairs covering its underside.

A

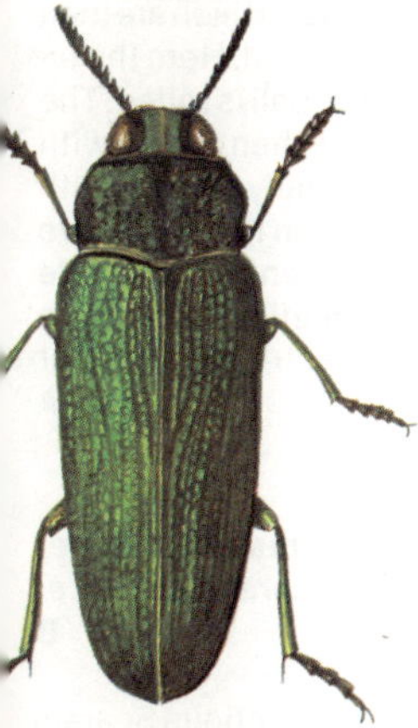

P. coronata

***Julodella* spp.** (Dusted Beetles) Beetles in the genus *Julodella* are rare and easily confused with the genus *Julodis*. Further information is required to assist in specific classification.

B

APRIL – MAY

Scarabaeoidea (Scarab Beetles)

The Scarabaeoidea is one of the largest superfamilies of insects, with over 20 000 species throughout the world. Adults are sturdily built and some have unusual protrusions on head and thorax which give them a forbidding appearance. This super-family includes species of Goliath Beetles and Hercules Beetles which are the heaviest and most bulky of known insects. The super-family is divided into 2 main divisions, each determined by the larval food-source. One division includes the Scarabs or Dung Beetles which feed on excreta.

***Scarabaeus sacer* Linnaeus** (Sacred Scarab) Common in Arabia, where swarms often follow herds of camels and sheep in the desert. They pounce on any fresh droppings, making them into balls which are then rolled to an area of relatively soft ground. Here the insect excavates a hole into which the ball is rolled. The female lays an egg in the ball which is then coated with a cement to delay dehydration and finally covered with earth. By this process the larvae, when hatched, have a ready source of nourishment sufficient for complete development. In some areas the beetle has become nocturnal to avoid attacks by Kestrels and other falcons. **A**

***Mnematium rotundipennis* Holdhaus** (Lesser Scarab) Has similar habits to *Scarabaeus sacer* (Sacred Scarab). **B**

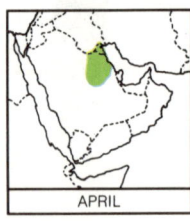

***Gymnopleurus mopsus* Pallas** (Pretentious Scarab) Has similar habits to *Scarabaeus sacer* (Sacred Scarab). **C**

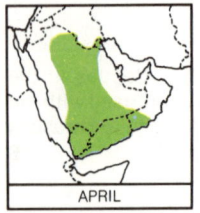

***Heliocopris gigas* Linnaeus** (Mighty Minotaur) The heaviest and largest Arabian beetle. In some males the head 'horns' or 'antlers' can reach 2 cm in height. Habits similar to *Scarabaeus sacer* (Sacred Scarab), but prefers cow droppings from which it makes balls. This preference limits habitat to areas where cows are kept. **D**

(Spiny Milk Vetch)

149

MARCH – AUGUST

***Pentodon algerinum* Herbst** (Lawn Beetle) Found in oases and grass-filled wadis, but has extended its habitat to gardens and lawns where, in many areas, it has become a pest. Larva, illustrated, typical of chafer division. Larvae live a subterranean existence, feeding on grass roots.

JANUARY – APRIL

***Schizonycha* spp.** (Desert Chafers) Several similar species of the genus *Schizonycha* are found in Arabia in desert areas with some grass. They have same habits as *Pentodon algerinum* (Lawn Beetle).

MARCH

***Phalangonyx arabicus* Arrow** (Arabian Chafer) Town suburbs and oasis farms are the habitats most frequented. Nocturnal and not often seen except when attracted by house lights at night.

MARCH – APRIL

***Phyllognathus excavatus* Forster** (Unicorn Beetle)
Larvae feed on decaying plant material, including rotting timber and saw dust. Adults often found under rocks, logs and debris.

APRIL – MAY

***Oryctes elegans* Prell** (Elegant Rhinoceros Beetle)
Three species of the genus *Oryctes,* which are similar in appearance, are widespread in Arabia, although *O. elegans* is the most common. They usually inhabit date palm oases and are nocturnal, but occasionally are attracted to house lights. Head adornment or horn is much more developed and prominent in the male.

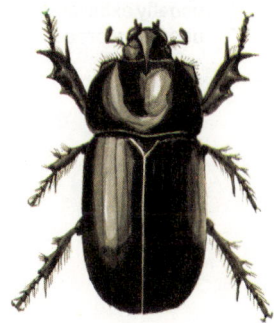

APRIL – JULY

***Rhyssemus granosus* Klug** (Wrinkly Beetle) There are several different species belonging to the genus *Rhyssemus* in Arabia, distinguishable by the pattern of wrinkles on the thorax. *Rhyssemus granosus* is the most common. Favourite haunts are gardens in town suburbs.

× 3.5

151

MARCH – APRIL

***Tropinota squallida* Scopoli** (Milkvetch Chafer)
Prefers open desert with rock-strewn wadis, where it is attracted to flowers of *Astragalus spinosus* (Spiny Milk Vetch).

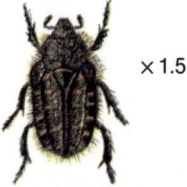

× 1.5

MARCH – APRIL

***Aphodius wallastoni* Harold** (Pale Dung Beetle)
Species belonging to the genus *Aphodius*, such as *A. wallastoni*, are common throughout Arabia where animal droppings are found. Different species are attracted by excreta of different animals. Most species are similar in appearance, with similar habits. The beetle does not attempt to move the droppings, but usually excavates a hollow beneath them, which is then used as a brood chamber.

× 1.5

Wadi Rasid, Saudi Arabia

Appendix: A new species of Mydaidae (Midas Flies)

***Rhopalia gyps* Bowden, sp.n.**   (Walker's Midas Fly) (See page 104)

Head mostly black, frons shining, antennal tubercle and clypeus light reddish-orange, eye margins narrowly and genae broadly dusted light yellow; hairs all light golden; antennae (illustrated) light orange-yellow, first segment with light yellowish hair; proboscis black, projecting to about middle of third antennal segment; frons at vertex slightly less than half width of head, slightly more than half at level of antennae, face narrowing to one third head width at lower buccal margin.

Thorax reddish-orange, shining; mesonotum with narrow, faint brown admedian stripes from anterior margin to post-alar calli and an even fainter brownish median stripe, notopleura vaguely brownish; meso-anepisternum brownish in middle, a black spot above middle coxa, 2 blackish spots between metathoracic spiracle and hind coxa, a black spot on latero-tergite immediately beneath squama; pubescence light yellowish to golden, very short and sparse on mesonotum and tending to concentrate along admedian stripes, longer and denser on notopleura, pleura bare except for sparse yellowish hair on pro-episternum, pro-epimeron and posterior margin of meso-epimeron; scutellum brownish-orange, basal corners black, a few golden hairs along extreme anterior margin.

Abdomen reddish-orange, black marks at extreme sides of second to seventh tergites, those on fifth to seventh contiguous with black marks on sternites, bullae black, longer diameter nine times shorter diameter; last four sternites with prominent black hind margins; pubescence yellowish to golden, very sparse and short, somewhat longer and denser on first tergite. Legs reddish-orange with concolorous spines and pubescence, claws black tipped, pulvilli yellowish, barely half length of claws. Wing (illustrated) brownish sub-hyaline, costal cell pale yellowish, prominent brown borders to all longitudinal veins except anal, centres of marginal and first basal cells only narrowly clear, axillary lobe entirely sub-hyaline, alula hyaline; costa yellow with black apex, other veins yellowish basally darkening to brownish-black apically; a cross vein present from third posterior cell to wing margin; squamae linear, opaquely whitish with very sparse, short yellowish fringe; haltere yellowish-orange. Genitalia; ninth tergite distinctly carinate, upper part of carina darkened, acanthophorites each with 6 orange spines. Length of body 14.5 mm, of wing 11.5 mm, of antennae 3.3 mm, of proboscis 2 mm.

Holotype ♀, Saudi Arabia: Riyadh, Mecca Road, vulture site, 2.May.1980 (D.H. Walker). In coll. D.H.W.

This species is similar to *R. annulata* Sack, from Syria, and *R. bequaerti* Lyneborg from Afghanistan, in possessing a cross vein from the third posterior cell to the posterior wing margin. *Rhopalia annulata* is a darker species, clypeus

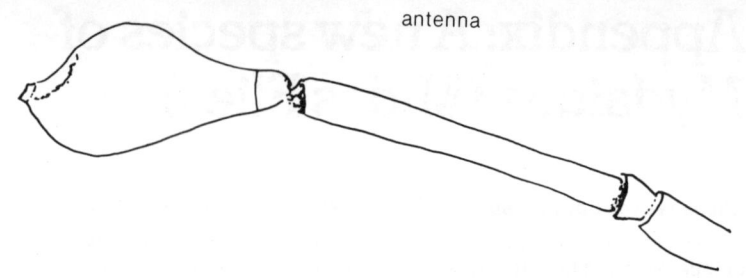

blackish-brown, mesonotum with a distinct black middle stripe and abdominal tergites with black anterior bands. *Rhopalia bequaerti* is yellowish, like *R. gyps,* but has clypeus brownish, pleura, except mesoanepisternum and laterotergite, and scutellum black, and sixth and seventh sternites black. In general appearance *R. gyps* is very similar to *R. tutankhameni* Brunetti, from the Sudan and Algeria, but is immediately distinguished by the cross vein in the hind margin of the wing.

This species is one of the first Mydaidae known from Saudi Arabia and the first from the more central area. Two other *Rhopalia* species and one species of *Leptomydas*, to be described elsewhere, are known from Jebel Daka and Mugheira in the northwest corner near the Jordanian border.

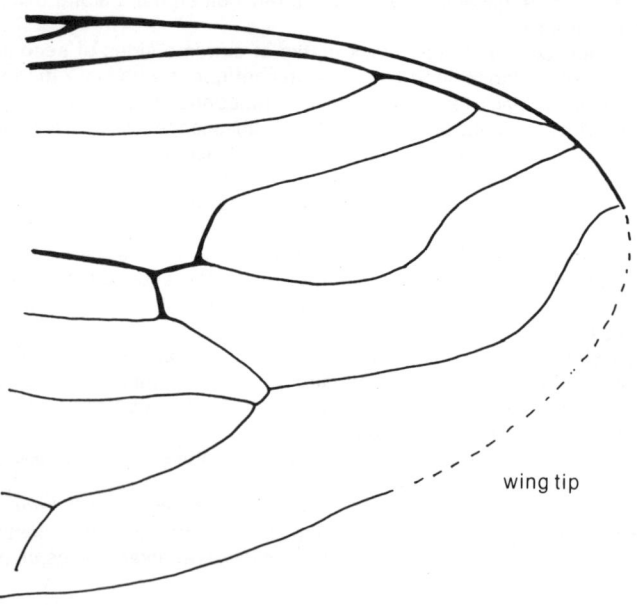

Reflections on Arabia

Below are given a series of tales from experiences encountered in Arabia during the writing of this book.

The expatriate

'Please fasten your seat belts and extinguish all cigarettes; in a few minutes you will be landing at Riyadh Airport'. There was a buzz of excited chatter as the passengers complied with the instructions and at the same time tried to obtain a first glimpse of their destination through the small windows of the aircraft. The newcomer looked around at his fellow travellers who were the nationals of many countries, and he also experienced their excitement. They then disembarked and the coach took them to passport control where they stood in orderly lines waiting to have their visas checked. There had been a few wives and families, but these had been attended to first; now the queue was mainly men. From a dozen different cultures with varying life-styles they were all here to work and to fill a multitude of jobs. After collecting his baggage and passing through customs he moved to the exit. Unable to speak Arabic, he wondered what he should do if there was no one present to meet him. But to his relief, above the jostling crowd, he saw a waving board with his name written on it.

He was driven through the thriving modern city to meet his new employers, then given a meal and shown to his apartments. His new home was comfortable and well appointed with modern air-conditioning units. The effects of jet lag and the completely different environment made him relax. It was then that he saw a flash of silver on the wall caused by the movement of a small insect, a Silverfish. Many times he had seen them on the wall of his cottage at home. A primitive little insect that is covered in shining, silver scales and lives in domestic homes where it feeds on tiny scraps of paper or spilt food. He watched with interest its passage up the wall, then cast his eyes out of the window half expecting to see the green fields and the sea in the distance. Instead he saw the outskirts of the town and the desert with the setting sun, a great round ball of fire whose lower rim had just touched the horizon. Fascinated, he timed its departure; it took precisely two minutes to slip out of sight. Then the sky changed colour from bright blue to different shades of mauve and the white clouds turned pink as they captured the last rays of the sun. Slowly this kaleidoscope of colour altered the scene, forming an unforgettable picture with the minaret of the mosque and a palm tree silhouetted against the deep red sky. He was deeply affected by the beauty of his new surroundings. The call to evening prayers drew him out of his reverie.

Jebel Tuwaiq, Saudi Arabia

It was bound to happen sooner or later

The day was hot, very hot, with the sun vertically overhead, and the reflected heat played tricks with the eyes. The horizon of the sand and rock desert disappeared into the Empty Quarter, with a lake and some palm trees quite clearly discernible in the foreground. A few minutes later and the mirage had disappeared, leaving a ridge of rocks and a few sparse acacias. But the large lake, half a mile away to the right, was not a mirage nor was the smaller one, a quarter of a mile to the left. A hot breeze caused the light to dance on the surface of Layla Lakes and it was painful to view them without wearing sunglasses; nevertheless they looked invitingly cool. The present predicament, however, gave no cause for poetic reflections.

The vehicle was only two feet from the hard track but all four wheels were immersed in soft sand, a problem that had been caused by misjudgement. After half an hour of digging and pushing, the situation had not improved and it was clear that more assistance would be necessary. Fortunately a pick-up truck containing a group of local young men came along the track; they pulled up, shook hands and a general discussion took place on how to solve the problem. Although the discussion was complicated by the different languages, a plan of action was agreed. All four tyres of the vehicle were deflated until they were only a quarter full of air. Then with one person driving and everybody else pushing, the vehicle regained the hard surface of the track. The whole party travelled to the cool of the lakeside where the new friendship was cemented by sharing fruit and drink.

The object of the visit was to collect dragonflies and this was explained to the young men by sign language. They led the way to a location where the banks were covered in tall grass. The water was clear and a shoal of fish swam past, while a Heron stood motionless among the reeds. Many different types of dragonfly were sighted, all of which are recorded in this book.

Fine fare

To the north of Riyadh lies Rumah, situated in the centre of a desert of rock and sand. The undulating country has small barren hills with very little vegetation even during the rainy season, and few animals live there except for the Dhub. The Dhub or Spiny-tailed Lizard looks prehistoric and can grow up to 60 cm (2 ft) in length. It has a small head, a fat body and a large tail covered in heavy spines. It feeds on the sparse vegetation and will venture some distance from its tunnel lair which is often situated in the side of a small hillock. When disturbed it moves very fast and soon disappears below ground. However, if cornered it presents a frightening appearance and the open mouth reveals sharp, white teeth, although it is the spiny tail that is usually used with devastating effect for defence.

A wadi winds its way across the landscape, discernible from a distance by the small groups of acacias and other shrubs that cling to the banks. It was a month since the last rain and it would probably be nine months before it rained again. The wadi was mainly dry by now, but by following its course isolated stretches of water could be discovered where the bed was deeper. Here the small shrubs and local plants were still green and visited by a host of insects. The birds searching the mud by the water's edge were a mixed flock of waders, mainly Redshanks and Sandpipers, while further up the bank a small number of Yellow Wagtails examined the flotsam left behind by the retreating water. Skimming the water, giving a dazzling exhibition of aerobatics as they banked and turned, was a flock of White Winged Black Terns in their summer plumage, an unforgettable sight of grace and beauty. On being approached, the Sandpipers began to bob up and down and finally the whole flock took to the air with startled cries, circled, and made their way across the desert to another temporary refuge from the approaching heat of summer.

An examination of the flotsam revealed many small beetles and other tiny forms of life providing food for a large number of earwigs in various stages of growth. When disturbed, the female earwigs demonstrated their maternal instinct and adopted offensive postures to defend their young, a characteristic which is remarkable of this insect.

A small plume of smoke rose above the trees further down the wadi and the smell of burning wood was borne on the hot breeze. Three men approached and after the customary greetings they were offered fruit and water. They were interested in the insects and birds. The use of the equipment was shown to them, but further discussion was limited due to the language barrier. They indicated the way to their camp, where seats were found around the fire. Food was being cooked in a large metal pot. When the lid was removed, a delicious aroma whetted the hungry appetites. Everyone ate his fill of saffron rice and the delicate tasting meat. Comfortably satisfied, the meal an undoubted success, a polite enquiry was made regarding the nature of the meat. The answer was Dhub.

Faisal

Faisal was his name — a sturdy boy aged about ten. As the eldest child he was a dutiful son and the secret pride of his father. It was late afternoon when he drove the herd of sheep along the wide track in Wadi Hanifah. The sun was behind him and the high midday temperatures had gone, but the air was still and close. There were approximately one hundred and fifty sheep in the flock, all with long black trailing coats and tails, which contrasted with their partially white faces. These animals are hardy and are well adapted to life in the desert. He had brought them some distance from a good grazing area and they were now travelling through a narrow and desolate gorge devoid of vegetation. Steep cliffs rose twenty metres on either side of the path. The sound of the many feet echoed faintly from the rocks and a small cloud of dust followed their progress.

The boy was happy at the prospect of being reunited with his family and enjoying the evening meal. It was then that he spotted the rope lying at the base of the cliff. The previous week his father had lost a rope; how pleased he would be to have it returned to him. Tossing his *goutra* (headgear) to one side of his head he left the flock and moved quickly to pick up the rope. As he approached he disturbed a large desert grasshopper which flew up in his face. The boy started, faltered, then froze as the rope uncurled and the snake confronted him. Motionless he watched as it slowly raised its head above the ground to eye him with an unflinching gaze. Beads of sweat formed on the boy's brow and he took one hesitant step backwards — the snake moved forward, then stopped. With fear gripping him, the boy took several more slow steps backwards — the snake once more followed. The boy cast his eyes around for a refuge, but the cliffs were bare and there was no place to retreat. The snake slowly slid towards the boy. The boy picked up his *thobe* (gown) turned and ran as fast as he could. In desperation he ran into the flock of sheep, bumping against their soft warm bodies. He did not check his flight until he had forced his way to the centre of the friendly animals; only then did he dare cast a glance over his shoulder to the path behind. The boy travelled in the midst of the sheep, long until that fearful place with its lone occupant was out of sight.

Farashah

The Land Rover was parked beside one of the acacia trees, but this provided little shade because the midday sun was vertically overhead. The tree was one of a dozen dotted here and there in the dry wadi. High cliffs rose sheer more than 150 metres above the jumbled mass of rocks that littered the sides of the wadi. The only sound came from two Fantail Ravens whose calls echoed on the timeless wind which had formed the grotesque shapes of the eroded summit. A few camels cropped quietly the leaves of the trees, their loose, soft mouths skilfully avoiding injury from the long thin thorns that clothed every branch. Beyond the wadi the stone desert stretched to the near horizon where a sand desert, deep red, merged its wind-blown contours and disappeared into the heat haze. The trees were in bloom, their bright yellow blossom adding a heavy but attractive scent to the hot breeze and was the source of attraction to a host of insects. Indentification of insect species among this lively group entailed their capture. This required considerable skill because one inaccurate sweep could result in the thorns capturing the net.

On the horizon a plume of dust travelled across the desert, marking the approach of a vehicle. When it arrived, the truck contained two men, handsome in their red check headgear and long white *thobes*. After the serious formality of shaking hands, they offered the expatriates water, an all-important commodity in such a place. Neither group spoke the other's language. However, after many polite refusals, all sat, drank the cool water, and ate fruit together. Then the use of the butterfly net was demonstrated, and a lovely insect with white wings and orange tips was caught. The Bedouin called this farashah, the expatriates called it butterfly. Its beauty was appreciated by everyone.

Riyadh farm

Diriyah, Saudi Arabia

The genie and the carpet

From the top of the escarpment the view was extensive; the cliffs stretched away on either side forming a giant wall of irregular outline broken by countless ravines and gorges plunging into the plateau behind. In front, the cliffs descended in sheer fall of 300 metres to the desert floor. From a land of mighty rocks and dry wadis to a sea of sand, here a vista of straight lines and unique shapes, there soft windswept contours and curves. In the intense heat there was no shade visible in any direction. The sky, a bright blue, faded as it met the land, giving an uncertainty to the horizon. A black Bedouin tent stood alone in the desert, pitched beneath an isolated pinnacle of rock. The scene was very beautiful with its pastel browns and reds, but had an air of unreality. It is in such conditions that the imagination has food for thought.

Out of the distant haze a movement was discernible, a swirling shape. The genie reached up from the ground and funnelled its white form into the clear blue sky, swaying as it moved rapidly towards the pinnacle of rock. When it reached this, a rectangular black object rose above the tent, before floating silently towards the escarpment. The heat and the haze of the background gave to this form the shape of an undulating carpet, which flew into one of the deep gorges of the escarpment. Its arrival was welcomed by an unearthly clamour of howls and cries which echoed like screams from the dozens of caves that honeycombed the cliffs. Such was the effect of heat and solitude, but reality was different.

The small whirlwind or 'dustdevil' had permitted the Griffon Vulture to rise on the thermals from the pinnacle of rock, whence it had flown in search of food, towards the gorge. This very large bird with wing span of 2 metres had disturbed a pack of wild dogs which were feeding off the carcass of a dead goat. The vulture was particularly unwelcome, as one of the bitches had left her litter of puppies unprotected. Barking, she had raced back to the small cave to find them safe, but hungry. Having fed them, the bitch turned her attention to other unwelcome visitors. Systematically she searched her fur and the puppies' fur for fleas. Most wild dogs are afflicted by these insects which are parasites that suck the dogs' blood.

Time and life

The first week it was the ravens and a movement among the rocks at the base of the escarpment that caught the eye. The stone desert, empty, hot and dry, extended in all directions from horizon to horizon until it met the cliffs of the escarpment. It was late summer and most of the plants were bare of leaves, dry and brittle, baked in the stifling heat. A few acacias still stood green, in stark contrast to the harshness of the season. The Brown Necked Ravens swooped low over the ground calling raucously to one another; the object of their attention was a solitary camel, a very old camel, which did not even look up when one of the uninvited visitors impudently landed on his back. Each plodding step was a deliberate effort, which caused the animal to sway as it searched for food within easy reach of its emaciated body. Its large eyes looked weary and sad. Gone were the days when it had run for hours with long stride carrying its master effortlessly across the desert, driving the herd of camels from one feeding ground to another. Now its days were numbered.

The second week the desert and escarpment appeared unchanged, but there was no movement and the ravens had gone. The hot breeze bore a pungent smell that emanated from the remains of the once proud beast, which was stretched out in its last resting place, its total energy spent. Nature now assisted in its final departure. The work had been started by the ravens, then a Steppe Eagle had visited the carcase and then a Desert Fox. The remains were alive with activity as several different species of beetle and fly made it their temporary home, rapidly feeding and breeding, each carrying out its duty in the web of life.

The third week the desert and escarpment still shimmered in the heat. A light breeze stirred the dried skin and white bones in their final resting place.

His Garden

So far, the trip had been a success. Many new species of insect were discovered in the area of farmland to the south. Now the route crossed a flat desert of sand completely devoid of vegetation. It stretched to the horizon and there were large areas of salt pan which reflected the sun's rays and hurt the eyes, but the real worry was fuel. At the last petrol station the needle of the fuel gauge had indicated a three-quarters full tank, but for the last ten minutes it had been flickering on the 'E' mark. Either the gauge was faulty or the tank was nearly empty; however, there was no other option than to motor on. The road climbed steeply to a barren, heat-baked plateau littered with boulders and outcrops of rock. This empty terrain was occasionally fissured with deep, dry wadis which did not look as if they had witnessed water from the day of their creation. It was most inhospitable country, very hot, devoid of shade and without any sign of life, and definitely not the place to run out of fuel. The decision to lighten the load by excluding the spare can of petrol was now regretted as the anxiety increased.

Then, after following the road around a rock outcrop, a most welcome sight was revealed — a house with one solitary petrol pump. Such good fortune was unbelievable. The owner was sitting in the shade drinking tea with a companion. When the petrol was supplied the car's gauge was proved to be faulty. It was only necessary to purchase half a tank of petrol to obtain full capacity. Having completed the transaction, the owner with traditional hospitality offered tea. Relieved of the fuel problem it was pleasant to relax in the relative cool shade of the house. The owner's companion, who was also dressed in traditional clothes, then asked in perfect English whether the tea was to 'your liking'. Replying that the tea was perfect, the recent petrol problem was explained; he

Riyadh, Saudi Arabia

then repeated this in Arabic to the owner. Everyone laughed, but ten minutes earlier the situation had appeared far from funny.

During the conversation, the object and results of the trip were discussed. The man then asked: 'Would you like to see my garden?' The word conjured up visions of green lawns and colourful flower beds. Looking at the sun-baked desert but not wishing to be impolite, the answer was given with an indulgent smile: 'Yes'. He replied: 'Follow me'. The pick-up truck turned off the road and for twenty minutes the route followed a dusty trail across the treeless rock desert until it finally arrived at a deep wadi. Here the track zigzagged down one hundred metres and passed through ancient tamarisk trees into what seemed like another world. Surrounded on either side by sheer cliffs, the way led through neat orange groves and a field of tall corn to the house which stood in the shade of date palms. A small, black Bedouin tent, open on all sides, was pitched on the grass in front of the house. He pulled up and led the way to the tent which contained a carpet, padded arm rests, brazier and cooking utensils.

Everyone sat comfortably on the carpet while he noisily ground coffee in a traditional gesture of welcome. Sipping the strong hot drink gave us time to reflect on the beauty of the surroundings. The whole area was green and there were small fields of different produce which included onions, radishes, aubergines and watermelons. Irrigation channels supplied water pumped from a distant well. Bright splashes of different colours were supplied by several large bushes of Bougainvillea. The air was alive with insects and the trees echoed with the sound of birds. A warm breeze blew through the tent carrying the sweet scent from a field of bright blue alfalfa. A large silver tray of dates and a huge bowl of fresh camel's milk was passed round the company. All agreed that this was a very fine garden.

Bibliography

Basilewsky, P. (1979). Insects of Saudi Arabia. Coleoptera: Fam. Carabidae. *Fauna of Saudi Arabia,* **I,** 141 – 146.

Bílý, S. (1979). Insects of Saudi Arabia. Coleoptera: Fam. Buprestidae. *Fauna of Saudi Arabia,* **I,** 215 – 222.

Bílý, S. (1980). Insects of Saudi Arabia. Coleoptera: Fam. Buprestidae (part 2). *Fauna of Saudi Arabia,* **2,** 119 – 121.

Bindagji, H.H. (1978). Atlas of Saudi Arabia. London.

Bodenheimer, F.S. (1951). *Citrus Entomology in the Middle East,* Holland.

Brancucci, M. (1979). Insects of Saudi Arabia. Coleoptera: Fam. Haliphidae, Dytiscidae, Gyrinidae. *Fauna of Saudi Arabia,* **I,** 156 – 161.

Brancucci, M. (1980). Insects of Saudi Arabia. Coleoptera: Fam. Haliplidae, Dytiscidae, Gryinidae (part 2). *Fauna of Saudi Arabia,* **2,** 102 – 111.

Büttiker, W., Attiah, M.D. and Pont, A.C. (1979). Insects of Saudi Arabia. Diptera: Synanthropic flies. *Fauna of Saudi Arabia,* **I,** 352 – 367.

Büttiker, W. (1980). Insects of Saudi Arabia. Diptera: Fam. Hippoboscidae. *Fauna of Saudi Arabia,* **2,** 338 – 340.

Chassain, J. (1979). Insects of Saudi Arabia. Coleoptera: Fam. Elateridae. *Fauna of Saudi Arabia,* **I,** 193 – 211.

Chhotani, O.B. and Bose, G. (1979). Insects of Saudi Arabia. Isoptera. *Fauna of Saudi Arabia,* **I,** 75 – 83.

Chinery, M. (1972). *A Field Guide to the Insects of Britain and northern Europe,* London.

Dlabola, J. (1979). Insects of Saudi Arabia. Homoptera. *Fauna of Saudi Arabia,* **I,** 115 – 139.

Dlabola, J. (1980). Insects of Saudi Arabia. Homoptera: Auchenorrhyncha (part 2). *Fauna of Saudi Arabia,* **2,** 74 – 94.

Endrödi, S. (1980). Insects of Saudi Arabia. Coleoptera: Fam. Scarabaeidae. *Fauna of Saudi Arabia,* **2,** 157 – 158.

Fürsch, H. (1979). Insects of Saudi Arabia. Coleoptera: Fam. Coccinellidae. *Fauna of Saudi Arabia,* **I,** 235 – 248.

Gabriel, A.G. (1954). Lepidoptera Rhopalocera. *Expedition to South-West Arabia, 1937 – 38,* **I,** 351 – 391.

Greathead, D.J. (1980). Insects of Saudi Arabia. Diptera: Fam. Bombyliidae. *Fauna of Saudi Arabia,* **2,** 291 – 337.

Greathead, D.J. (1980). Beeflies (Bombyliidae, Diptera) from Oman. *J. Oman Studies,* **2,** 233 – 250.

Heinetz, R. (1979). Insects of Saudi Arabia. Coleoptera: Fam. Carabidae. *Fauna of Saudi Arabia,* **I,** 140.

Heinzel, H., Fitter, R. and Parslow, J. (1972). *The Birds of Britain and Europe with North Africa and the Middle East,* London.

Higgins, L.C. and Riley, N.D. (1970). *A Field Guide to the Butterflies of Britain and Europe,* London.

Hölzel, H. (1980). Insects of Saudi Arabia. Neuroptera: Fam. Chrysopidae. *Fauna of Saudi Arabia,* **2,** 164 – 173.

Hyde, G.E. (1961). *Entomology,* London.

Kaszab, Z. (1979). Insects of Saudi Arabia. Coleoptera: Fam. Teneorionidae. *Fauna of Saudi Arabia*, I, 257 – 288.

Kaszab, Z. (1981). Insects of Saudi Arabia. Coleoptera: Fam. Tenebrionidae (part 3). *Fauna of Saudi Arabia*, 3, 276 – 407.

Kryzhanovskij, O. (1979). Insects of Saudi Arabia. Coleoptera: Fam. Histeridae. *Fauna of Saudi Arabia*, I, 184 – 185.

Larsen, T.B. (1974). *Butterflies of Lebanon*, Beirut.

Larsen, T.B. (1977). The butterflies of eastern Oman and their zoogeographic composition. *J. Oman Studies*, I, 179 – 208.

Larsen, T.B. (1980). The butterflies of Dhofar and their zoogeographic composition. *J. Oman Studies*, I,153 – 186.

Larsen, T.B. and Larsen, K. (1980). *Butterflies of Oman*, London.

Larsen, T.B. and Pittaway, A.R. (1982). Notes on the ecology, biology and taxonomy of Apharitis acamas (Klug) (Lep: Lycaenidae). *Entomologist's Gaz.*, 33, 163 – 168.

Lipscombe-Vincett, B.A. (1977). *Wild flowers of central Saudi Arabia*, Milan.

Lipscombe-Vincett, B.A. (1982). *Animal Life in Saudi Arabia*, Italy.

Mandaville, J.P. (1977). Plants. *J. Oman Studies*, I, 229 – 267.

Mandl, K. (1980). Insects of Saudi Arabia. Coleoptera: Fam. Carabidae. *Fauna of Saudi Arabia*, 2, 95 – 101.

Migahid, A.M. and Hammouda, M.A. (1974). *Flora of Saudi Arabia*, Riyadh.

Mroczkowski, M. (1979). Insects of Saudi Arabia. Coleoptera: Fam. Dermestidae. *Fauna of Saudi Arabia*, I, 212 – 214.

Panlian, R. (1980). Insects of Saudi Arabia. Coleoptera: Fam. Scarabaeoidea. *Fauna of Saudi Arabia*, 2, 141 – 154.

Pelham-Clinton, E.C. (1977). Pyralidae from Oman. *J. Oman Studies*, I, 177 – 178.

Pitcher, D.A. (1979). Some observations on the insects of the eastern province of Saudi Arabia. Part 1: Lepidoptera. *J. Saudi Arabian nat. Hist. Soc.*, 24, 16 – 25.

Pittaway, A.R. (1979). The butterflies and hawkmoths of eastern Saudi Arabia. *Proc. Br. ent. nat. Hist. Soc.*, 12, 90 – 101.

Pittaway, A.R. (1980). Butterflies (Lepidoptera) of Qatar, April – June (1979). *Entomologist's Gaz.*, 31, 103 – 111.

Pittaway, A.R. (1981). Further notes on the butterflies and hawkmoths (Lepidoptera) of eastern Saudi Arabia. *Entomologist's Gaz.*, 32, 27 – 35.

Pittaway, A.R. (1983). The Dragons of Al-Hasa (Odonata). *Aramco World Magazine*, 2, 2 – 3.

Popov, G.B. (1980). Acridoidea of Eastern Arabia. *J. Oman Studies*, 2, 113 – 148.

Radcliffe-Smith, A. (1980). The vegetation of Dhofar. *J. Oman Studies*, 2, 59 – 86.

Roche, C.G. (1981). Notes on the bees and wasps of the U.A.E. *Bull. Emirates nat. Hist. Group*, 15, 12 – 20.

Smart, P. (1976). *The Illustrated Encyclopedia of the Butterfly World in Colour*, London.

Stanek, V.J. (1969). *The Pictorial Encyclopedia of Insects*, London.

Stork and Renouf (1932). *Fundamentals of Biology*, London.

Tweedie, M. (1977). *Insect Life*, London.

Waterston, A.R. (1980). Insects of Saudi Arabia. Odonata. *Fauna of Saudi Arabia*, 2, 57 – 70.

Wiltshire, E.P. (1952). Lepidoptera recently taken in Arabia. *Bull. Soc. Fouad i. Ent.*, **36,** 135 – 174.

Wiltshire, E.P. (1961). A new genus, eight new species, seven new forms and notes on the Lepidoptera of Saudi Arabia, Bahrain and Iran. *J. Bombay nat. Hist. Soc.*, **58,** 608 – 631.

Wiltshire, E.P. (1964). The Lepidoptera of Bahrain. *J. Bombay nat. Hist. Soc.*, **59,** 779 – 799.

Wiltshire, E.P. (1964). The Lepidoptera of Bahrain. *J. Bombay nat. Hist. Soc.*, **61,** 119 – 141.

Wiltshire, E.P. (1977). Lepidoptera: Part I. *J. Oman Studies*, **I,** 155 – 160.

Wiltshire, E.P. (1977). A list of further Lepidoptera Heterocera from Oman. *J. Oman Studies*, **2,** 233 – 250.

Wiltshire, E.P. (1980). Insects of Saudi Arabia. Lepidoptera. *Fauna of Saudi Arabia*, **2,** 179 – 240.

Index of Scientific Names

THYSANURA
Lepismatidae
   Thermobia domestica   2

ODONATA

ZYGOPTERA
Platycnemididae
   Arabicnemis caerulea   4
Coenagriidae
   Ischnura evansi   5
   Enallagma vansomereni   5
   Ceriagrion glabrum   6

ANISOPTERA
Gomphidae
   Lindenia tetraphylla   6
Aeshnidae
   Anax imperator   6
   A.parthenope   6
   Hemianax ephippiger   8
Libellulidae
   Diplacodes lefebvrei   8
   Orthetrum sabina   8
   O.taeniolatum   8
   O.chrysostigma   8
   Trithemis annulata   10
   T.kirbyi   10
   T.arteriosa   10
   Pantala flavescens   10
   Selysiothemis nigra   10
   Crocothemis erythraea   12
   C.chaldaeorum   12

ORTHOPTERA or SALTATORIA
Gryllotalpidae
   Gryllotalpa gryllotalpa   14
Gryllidae
   Acheta domestica   14
   Gryllus bimaculatus   15
Tettigoniidae
   Phaneroptera sparsa   16
Acrididae
   Anacridium aegyptium   16
   Locusta migratoria   16
   Schistocerca gregaria   16
   Truxalis procera   18
   Aiolopus thalassinus   18
   Ochrilidia gracilis   18
   Pyrgomorpha conica   18
   Morphacris fasciata   18
   Heteracris littoralis   20
   Sphingonotus rubescens   20
   Pseudosphingonotus savignyi   20
   Poekilocerus bufonius   20
   Utubius syriacus   20
Tetrigidae
   Hedotettix alienus   22
   Paratettix ocellatus   22

DERMAPTERA
Labiduridae
   Labidura riparia   23

DICTYOPTERA
Blattidae
   Periplaneta americana   24
   Blatella germanica   24
   B.mellea   24
   Blatta orientalis   26
   B.lateralis   26
Mantidae
   Blepharopsis mendica   26
   Empusa hedenborgi   26
   Hypsicorypha gracilis   26
   Mantis religiosa   28
   Oxyothespis nilotica   28
   Eremiaphila braueri   28

ISOPTERA
Rhinotermitidae
   Psammotermes hybostoma   30

PSOCOPTERA
(Species not included in this book)

MALLOPHAGA
(Species not included in this book)

ANOPLURA
Pediculidae
   Pediculus humanus capitis   31
   P.h.humanus   31
   Phthirus pubis   31

HEMIPTERA

HETEROPTERA
Miridae
   Deraeocoris pallens   33
Cydnidae
   Macroscytus brunneus   34
Pentatomidae
   Nezara viridula   34
   Eysarcoris inconspicuus   34
Dinidoridae
   Coridius viduatus   34
Cimicidae
   Cimex lectularius   35
Rhopalidae
   Liorhyssus hyalinus   36
Alydidae
   Mirperus jaculus   36
Lygaeidae
   Dieuches mucronatus   36
   Lygaeus equestris   36
Naucoridae
   Heleocoris minusculus   37
Nepidae
   Laccotrephes fabricii   38
Notonectidae
   Anisops debilis   38

HOMOPTERA
Cicadidae
   Platypleura arabica   38
   Psalmocharias flavicollis   40
   Melampsalta musiva   40
Dictyopharidae
   Philotheria spp.   40
Aphididae
   Myzus persicae   40
   Aphis nerii   41

THYSANOPTERA
Aeolothripidae
   Aeolothrips deserticola   42

NEUROPTERA
Ascalaphidae
   Bubopsis hamata   43
Nemopteridae
   Halter halteratus   44
   Dielocroce spp.   44
Chrysopidae
   Chrysoperla carnea   44
Myrmeleontidae
   Gepus invisus   45
   Lopezus fedtschenkoi   46
   Palpares dispar   46
   Myrmecaelurus laetus   46
   Ganguilus pallescens   46
   Centroclisis cervina   46
   Nophis teillardi   47

LEPIDOPTERA
Sphingidae
   Acherontia styx   48
   A.atropos   48
   Agrius convolvuli   50
   Macroglossum stellatarum   50
   Daphnis nerii   52
   Hyles livornica   52
   Hippotion celerio   54
   Cephonodes hylas   54
Noctuidae
   Agrotis sardzeana   55
   A.ipsilon   55
   Euxoa canariensis   55
   Discestra sociabilis   56
   Mythimna loreyi   56
   Metopoceras omar   56
   M.delicata   56
   Spodoptera littoralis   57
   S.exigua   57
   S.cilium   57
   Hadjina viscosa   57
   Rhabinopteryx subtilis   57
   Dysmilichia bicolor   58
   Heliothis nubigera   58
   H.armigera   58
   H.peltigera   58
   Rhodocleptria incarnata   59
   Masalia albida   59
   Acontia biskrensis   59
   A.lucida   59
   Chrysodeixis chalcites   59
   Cornutiplusia circumflexa   60

Trichoplusia ni	60
Earias vittella	60
Dysgonia torrida	60
Remigia frugalis	61
Ophiusa tirhaca	61
Clytie benenotata	61
C.sancta	61
Heteropalpia exarata	62
Pericyma signata	62
Tytroca fasciolata	62
Gnamptonyx innexa	62
Drasteria habibazel	62
Rhynchodontodes revolutalis	63
Anumeta asiatica	63
A.hilgerti	63
Acrobyla kneuckeri	63
Drasteriodes limata	63
Armada panaceorum	64
Emmelia trabealis	64
Autophila cymaenotaenia	64
Thria robusta	64
Cerocala sana	65
Arctiidae	
Utetheisa pulchella	65
Spilosoma arabica	65
Lymantriidae	
Casama innotata	66
Euproctis cervina	66
Lasiocampidae	
Chondrostega fasciata	66
Chilena laristana	67
Autosphyla henkei	67
Lasiocampa serrula	68
Streblote siva	68
Geometridae	
Pingasa lahayei	69
Hyperythra muselmana	69
Chlorissa discessa	69
Tephrina disputaria	70
Gnophos subvariegatus	70
Epirrhoe wiltshirei	70
Zamarada hyalinaria	70
Hemidromodes sabulifera	70
Lithostege notata	71
L.palaestinensis	71
Eupithecia ultimaria	71
Rhodometra sacraria	71
Cossidae	
Holcocerus gloriosus	72
Lamellocossus aries	72
Pterophoridae	
Emmelina monodactyla	72
Pyralidae	
Ephestia kuehniella	73
Nomophila noctuella	73
Lamoria anella	73
Cornifrons ulceratalis	73
Hesperiidae	
Coeliades anchises	74
Spialia doris	74
Gomalia elma	74
Gegenes nostrodamus	75
Pelopidas thrax	75
P.mathias	75
Papilionidae	
Papilio machaon	76
P.demoleus	76
Pieridae	
Artogeia rapae	78
A.krueperi	78
Elphinstonia charlonia	78
Euchloe belemia	79
E.falloui	79
E.aegyptiaca	79
Pontia daplidice	80
P.glauconome	80
Anaphaeis aurota	80
Colotis calais	82
C.phisadia	82
C.halimede	82
C.danae	83
C.liagore	83
C.fausta	84
C.chrysonome	84
Catopsilia florella	84
Eureme hecabe	84
Colias croceus	86
Lycaenidae	
Apharitis acamas	87
A.myrmecophila	87
Myrina silenus	88
Deudorix livia	88
Lampides boeticus	88
Pseudophilotes vicrama	88
P.abencerragus	88
Tarucus rosaceus	90
T.balkanicus	90
Azanus ubaldus	90
A.jesous	90
Anthene amarah	90

Zizeeria karsandra	92
Zizula hylax	92
Plebejus pylaon	92
Agrodiaetus loweii	92
Chilades parrhasius	92
C.galba	94
Freyeria trochylus	94
Nymphalidae	
Melitaea persea	94
Hypolimnas misippus	94
Junonia orithya cheesmani	96
J.o.here	96
J.hierta	96
Vanessa cardui	98
Satyridae	
Ypthima bolanica	98
Y.asterope	98
Neohipparchia parisatis	98
Danaidae	
Danaus chrysippus	100

DIPTERA

NEMATOCERA
Culicidae	
Culex pipiens	102
Anopheles spp.	102
Chironomidae	
Chironomus dorsalis	102

BRACHYCERA
Tabanidae	
Tabanus mordax	103
T.rupinae	103
T.polygonus	103
Therevidae	
Hoplosathe frauenfeldi	104
Conopidae	
Conops nubeculipennis	104
Mydaidae	
Rhopalia gyps	104
Asilidae	
Apoclea femoralis	105
Bombyliidae	
Cytherea alexandrina	105
Parachistus pulchellus	105
Anastoechus trisignatus	106

CYCLORRHAPHA
Drosophilidae	
Drosophila melanogaster	106
Tephritidae	
Dacus longistylus	106
Trupanea amoena	107
Ephydridae	
Ephydra flavipes	107
Syrphidae	
Paragus compeditus	107
Metasyrphus luniger	107
Eristalinus aeneus	108
E.megacephalus	108
Calliphoridae	
Lucilia sericata	108
Wohlfahrtia nuba	108
Chrysomya albiceps	109
C.regalis	109
Sarcophaga ruficornis	109
Muscidae	
Musca domestica	110
Hippoboscidae	
Hippobosca longipennis	110

SIPHONAPTERA
Pulicidae	
Pulex irritans	111
Ctenocephalides canis	111

HYMENOPTERA
Sphecidae	
Stizus vespoides	113
S.marnonis	114
S.bizonatus	114
Cerceris tricolorata	114
C.straminea	114
Bembex dahlbomi	115
Philanthus triangulum	115
Prionyx crudelis	115
Sceliphron madraspatanum	116
Sphex fumicatus	116
Parapsammophila turanica	116
Podalonia tydei	116
Scoliidae	
Scolia flavifrons	117
S.erythrocephala	117
Campsomeriella thoracica	117
Eumenidae	
Delta dimidiatipenne	118
D.campaniforme	118
Rhynchium oculatum	118
Euodynerus excellens	118
Chlorodynerus spp.	119

Vespidae
- Vespa orientalis — 120
- Polistes wattii — 120

Pompilidae
- Cyphononyx bretonii — 121
- Batozonellus fuliginosus — 121
- Mygnimia dorsalis — 121

Chrysididae
- Chrysis ehrenbergi — 122
- Stilbum cyanurum — 122

Formicidae
- Camponotus xerxes — 123
- C. sericeus — 123
- Cataglyphis niger — 123

Apoidea
- Xylocopa aestuans — 125
- Xylocopa spp. — 125
- Paracrocisa sinaitica — 125
- Amegilla nubica — 126
- A. byssina — 126
- Paramegilla semirufa — 126
- Anthophora extricata — 126
- Apis mellifera — 127
- Pseudapsis nilotica — 127
- Eucera dimidiata — 127
- Icteranthidium ferrugineum — 127
- Chalicodoma rubripes — 128
- Chalicodoma spp. — 128
- Coelioxys afra — 128
- Halictus seladonius — 128

COLEOPTERA

Carabidae
- Anthia duodecimguttata — 130
- Graphipterus minutus — 130
- Scarites guineensis — 130
- Bembidion saxatile — 131
- Chlaenius canariensis — 131
- Brachinus nobilis — 131
- Calosoma imbricatum — 132

Cicindelidae
- Myriochile melancholica — 132

Dytiscidae
- Guignotus major — 133
- Laccophilus pictipennis — 133
- Hyphydrus pictus — 133
- Cybister tripunctatus — 133
- Eretes sticticus — 134
- Prodaticus pictus — 134

Hydrophilidae
- Hydrous mesopotamiae — 134
- Hydrophilus aculeatus — 134

Nitidulidae
- Nitidula ciliata — 135

Meloidae
- Nemognatha chrysomelina — 135
- Mylabris gratiosa — 135
- Croscherichia richteri — 136

Coccinellidae
- Henosepilachna elaterii — 136
- Coccinella undecimpunctata — 136
- C. septempunctata — 136
- Adonia variegata — 137

Curculionidae
- Ammocleonus aschabadensis — 137
- Bothynoderes anxius — 137
- Sitophilus granarius — 137

Elateridae
- Aeoloides grisescens — 138

Histeridae
- Saprinus ornatus — 138
- S. uvarovi — 138

Cleridae
- Necrobia rufipes — 139

Dermestidae
- Anthrenus flavipes — 139
- Dermestes lardarius — 139
- D. frischii — 139

Silvanidae
- Oryzaephilus mercator — 140

Bruchidae
- Callosobruchus maculatus — 140

Tenebrionidae
- Micipsa spp. — 140
- Opatroides punctulatus — 141
- Opatropsis hispida — 141
- Pimelia arabica — 141
- Pimelia spp. — 141
- Tenebrio molitor — 142
- Tribolium castaneum — 142
- Ocnera hispida — 142
- Thriptera crinita — 142
- Blaps kollari — 143
- Adesmia cancellata — 143
- A. stoeckleini — 143
- A. cothurnata — 143
- Tentyrina palmeri — 144
- Mesostena puncticollis — 144

- *Paraplatyope arabica* — 144
- *Oxycara* spp. — 144
- *Zophosis punctata* — 144
- *Z. complanata* — 145
- *Erodius octocostatus* — 145
- *Scleron sulcatum* — 145
- *Prionotheca coronata* — 145

Buprestidae
- *Capnodis excisa* — 146
- *Steraspis speciosa* — 146
- *Sphenoptera faragi* — 146
- *Julodis euphratica* — 146
- *Julodella* spp. — 147

Scarabaeoidea
- *Scarabaeus sacer* — 148
- *Mnematium rotundipennis* — 148
- *Gymnopleurus mopsus* — 148
- *Heliocopris gigas* — 148
- *Pentodon algerinum* — 150
- *Schizonycha* spp. — 150
- *Phalangonyx arabicus* — 150
- *Phyllognathus excavatus* — 151
- *Oryctes elegans* — 151
- *Rhyssemus granosus* — 151
- *Tropinota squallida* — 151
- *Aphodius wallastoni* — 151

Index of Common Names

This is an alphabetical list of vernacular English names. Adjectives are placed at the beginning of the insect name, as spoken, e.g. Emerald Cuckoo Wasp, *not* Wasp, Emerald Cuckoo; but the definite article, where used, is positioned at the end of the name and in parentheses, e.g. Highwayman (The).

Acacia Looper,	70
Acacia Tussock Moth,	66
Aden Skipper,	74
African Babul Blue,	90
African Mallow Skipper,	74
African Migrant,	84
African Ringlet	98
American Cockroach,	24
Ant Domino,	130
Arabian Chafer,	150
Arabian Cicada,	38
Arabian Darkling Beetle,	141
Arabian Ermine,	65
Arabian Goatmoth,	72
Arabian Lobetail,	6
Arabian Paper Wasp,	120
Asian Grass Blue,	92
Asiatic Sand Moth,	63
Autumn Sword Grass,	55
Azure Skimmer,	8
Baluchi Ringlet,	98
Banded Cloak,	20
Banded Spider Wasp,	121
Bath White,	80
Baton Blue,	88
Beaded Runner,	132
Bedbug,	35
Bee Wolf,	115
Big Headed Dronefly,	108
Black-tipped Digger,	114
Bleached Ground Bug,	36
Bloodied Oil Beetle,	135
Blossom Bee,	126
Blue Pansy (cheesmani),	96
Blue Pansy (here),	96
Blue-shinned Grasshopper,	20
Blue-banded Ishnura,	5
Blue-spotted Arab,	82
Body Louse,	31
Bordered Straw,	58
Brass Plusia,	60
Brilliant Ground Beetle,	131
Bronze Ruby Tail,	122
Brown Spotted Lesser Leafworm,	57
Brown Trog,	34
Brown-veined White,	80
Brown White Spot,	62
Burnt Speck,	64
Burnt Thorn,	69
Canary Carpenter Bee,	125
Canary Island Dart,	55
Canary Vapourer,	66
Carcass Beetle,	139
Carmine Darter,	12
Carpenter Bee,	125
Carrion Beetle,	135
Chafer Wasp,	117
Check Capsid,	33
Checkerspot Fly,	108
Churchyard Beetle(s),	143
Cinereous Wasp,	116
Citrus Swallowtail,	76
Clouded Yellow,	86
Coffee and Cream Moth,	60
Coffee Clearwing,	54
Common Cockroach,	26
Common Cyclops Termite,	30
Common Grass Yellow,	84
Common Ground Mantis,	28
Common Mosquito,	102
Common Sand Wasp,	116
Common Swallowtail,	76
Common Ulcer,	73
Convolvulus Hawkmoth,	50
Copra Beetle,	139
Cotton Leafworm,	57
Cowardly Bee Fly,	106
Crab Louse,	31
Creamcake,	63
Crimson Speckled Footman,	65

Dark Clover,	58
Dark Sand Moth,	63
Dark Snout,	62
Dark Sword Grass,	55
Darkling Beetle,	141
Desert Annulet,	70
Desert Chafer(s),	150
Desert Darter,	10
Desert Giant Ant,	123
Desert Knotgrass Eggar,	67
Desert Knotweed Beetle,	146
Desert Leopard Butterfly,	87
Desert Locust,	16
Desert Runner,	123
Desert Thrips,	42
Desert White,	80
Diadem,	94
Dimorphic Cockroach,	26
Diving Pill,	133
Dog Flea,	111
Dog Ked,	110
Domino Bee,	125
Domino Beetle,	130
Dusky Hoverer,	105
Dusky Jewel,	146
Dusky Tip,	107
Dusted Beetle(s),	147
Eastern Death's-Head Hawkmoth,	48
Egyptian Tree Locust,	16
Elegant Antlion,	46
Elegant Ground Weevil,	137
Elegant Rhinoceros Beetle,	151
Elevated Stalker,	143
Eleven-spot Ladybird,	136
Emerald Beetle,	146
Emerald Cuckoo Wasp,	122
Emperor Dragonfly,	6
Eremic Cockroach,	24
Ermine Leopard,	72
Eyed Ladybird,	136
Fairy Mantis,	28
Fake Flour Beetle,	141
False Baton Blue,	88
False Beetle Wasp,	114
False Greenbottle,	109
False Wainscot,	59
Fawn Diving Beetle,	134
Figtree Blue,	88

Firebrat,	2
Flour Beetle,	142
Gaica Blue,	92
Gangling Grasshopper,	18
Gaudy Carpet Beetle,	139
German Cockroach,	24
Giant Beetle Wasp,	117
Giant Gem,	59
Giant Sand Swimmer,	145
Giant Skipper,	74
Girdled Skimmer,	8
Globe Skimmer,	10
Glossy Hoverfly,	107
Glossy Mining Bee,	128
Golden Arab,	84
Golden Tailed Ant,	123
Grain Weevil,	137
Grass Jewel,	94
Grass Pest,	18
Gravel Hopper,	22
Greater Tiger,	107
Green Lacewing,	44
Green Midge,	102
Green Plant Bug,	34
Green Striped White,	79
Greenish Black Tip,	78
Grey Eggar,	68
Grey Feathered Moth,	72
Grey Flower Bee,	126
Grey Gadfly,	103
Grey Horsefly,	103
Grey Longhorn Bee,	127
Grey Slipper,	73
Grey Swiftwing,	71
Gulley Darter,	10
Hairy Antlion,	46
Harlequin Ground Bug,	36
Harlequin Potter Wasp,	118
Head Louse,	31
Hejaz Thickhead,	104
Helmeted Mantis,	26
Herbage Bug,	34
Highwayman (The),	105
Hispid Beetle,	141
Hollow Grasshopper,	18
Honey Bee,	127
Hornet Digger,	113
House Cricket,	14

Housefly,	110
Human Flea,	111
Human Louse,	31
Hummingbird Hawkmoth,	50
Hunchback Antlion (The),	45
Irish Coffee,	58
Jasmine Emerald,	69
Joker (The),	105
Jujube Lappet,	68
Knotted Halterwing,	44
Krueper's Small White,	78
Labyrinth Moth,	65
Lappet Mantis,	26
Larder Beetle,	139
Lawn Beetle,	150
Layered Moth,	62
Layla Damselfly,	5
Leaden Ciliate Blue,	90
Lederers Cupid,	94
Leopard Oil Beetle,	135
Leopard Butterfly,	87
Lesser Emperor,	6
Lesser Leafworm,	57
Lesser Millet Skipper,	75
Lesser Mud Bee,	128
Lesser Scarab,	148
Lesser Wanderer,	100
Lined Snout,	63
Little Tiger Blue,	90
Locust Terror,	115
Loew's Blue,	92
Longlegged Antlion,	46
Long-tailed Blue,	88
Lucid Four Spot,	59
Malaria Mosquito(es),	102
Marblecake Moth,	62
Marbled Moth,	62
Masked Stiletto Fly,	104
Mediterranean Flour Moth,	73
Mediterranean Tiger Blue,	90
Melancholic Tiger Beetle,	132
Melon Bug,	34
Merchant Grain Beetle,	140
Metallic Ground Beetle,	131
Mighty Minotaur,	148
Migratory Locust,	16
Milkvetch Chafer,	152
Milkweed Aphid,	41
Milkweed Toadi,	20
Millet Skipper,	75
Miniature Diving Beetle,	133
Mole Cricket,	14
Mosquito (Common),	102
Mottled Diving Beetle,	133
Mouldy Straw,	59
Mud Bee,	126
Mud Dauber Wasp,	116
Ni Moth,	60
Nocturnal Ground Beetle(s),	140
Nubian Flower Bee,	126
Nubian Straw,	58
Oasis Skimmer,	8
Oasis Streak,	61
Ochre Hindwing,	61
Okra Pea Moth,	60
Oleander Hawkmoth,	52
Olive Eyes,	6
Olive Wasp Digger,	115
Opossum Beetle,	144
Orange Darter,	10
Orange Flushed Cicada,	40
Orange Legged Skip-Jack,	138
Orange Patch White,	82
Orange Wings,	121
Oriental Wasp,	120
Ornate Undertaker,	138
Painted Lady,	98
Pale Bush Cricket,	16
Pale Dung Beetle,	152
Pale Slant Face,	18
Peach and Potato Aphid,	40
Peaty Skipper,	75
Pellet Beetle(s),	144
Persian Fritillary,	94
Pigmy Backswimmer,	38
Pink Carpet,	70
Pink Panther,	56
Pinstriped Ground Weevil,	137
Pitted Beetle,	143
Plain Tiger,	100
Platinum Water Beetle,	134
Polkadot Antlion,	46

Name	Page
Polkadot Diving Beetle,	134
Pomegranate Playboy,	88
Powderblue Damselfly,	5
Praying Mantis,	28
Pretentious Scarab,	148
Purple Blushed Darter,	10
Purple Darter,	8
Pyrites Shorefly,	107
Rack Beetle,	144
Red Headed Beetle Wasp,	117
Red Mason Wasp,	118
Red Potter Wasp,	118
Red Spotted Undertaker,	138
Red Streak,	66
Regal Bluebottle,	109
Ringed Digger,	114
Rock Moth,	64
Rubbed Wing,	70
Rufous Bombardier Beetle,	131
Rufous Fleshfly,	109
Rush Veneer,	73
Rust Red Flour Beetle,	142
Sabre Toothed Beetle,	130
Sacred Scarab,	148
Sahel Orange Tip,	83
Salmon Arab,	84
Sand Swimmer,	145
Savile Row Beetle,	144
Scalloped Pug,	71
Scarce Green Striped White,	79
Scarce Stalker,	142
Scarlet Darter,	12
Scarlet Tip,	83
Serpent (The),	47
Seven-spot Ladybird,	136
Shadow (The),	116
Shadow Moth,	63
Shady Shades,	61
Shimmerwings,	57
Shiny Dronefly,	108
Short Legged Diving Beetle,	133
Short Legged Stalker,	142
Silver-striped Hawkmoth,	54
Single-line Wainscot,	56
Small Cupid,	92
Small Saucer Bug,	37
Small White,	78
Snow Leopard,	56
Sodom's Apple Fruit Fly,	106
Sooty Cheek,	18
Spider Witch,	121
Spiny Tail,	134
Spiny Tailed Bee,	128
Spotted Bean Weevil,	140
Spotted Sulphur,	64
Streaky Wing,	46
Stretched Water Scorpion,	38
Striped Grey,	57
Striped Hawkmoth,	52
Striped Mantis,	26
Striped Swiftwing,	71
Sulphurous Jewel Beetle,	146
Swamp Hopper,	22
Syrian Thickthigh,	20
Tawny Earwig,	23
Thickneck,	64
Threadwings,	44
Tiger Cicada,	40
Tippler Moth,	67
Topaz Arab	82
Tropical Field Cricket,	15
Two-toned Horsefly,	103
Two-toned Mason Wasp,	118
Ugly Trox,	145
Unicorn Beetle,	151
Unicorn Hopper(s),	40
Urchin Beetle,	145
Vagrant Emperor,	8
Variable Blushing Bug,	36
Variable Four Spot,	59
Variable Stalker,	143
Variegated Laydbird,	137
Velvet Spotted Blue,	90
Vestal,	71
Vinegar Fly,	106
Walker's Midas Fly,	104
Wasp Bee,	127
Wasp Oil Beetle,	136
Western Death's-Head Hawkmoth,	48
White Spotted Nutmeg,	56
White-edged Rock-Brown,	98
Whizz Beetle,	144
Willow Beauty,	69
Wiltshire's Carpet,	70

Winter Greenbottle,	108	Yellow Hindwing,	61
Wood White,	79	Yellow Mason Wasp,	119
Wrinkly Beetle,	151	Yellow Pansy,	96
		Yellow Streak,	20
Yellow Dagger,	36		
Yellow Digger,	114	Zebra Bee,	127
Yellow Fleck,	43	Zephyr Blue,	92
Yellow Flower Bee,	126		